COLOURS
OF THE
CAGE

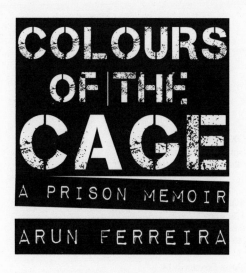

# COLOURS OF THE CAGE

## A PRISON MEMOIR

### ARUN FERREIRA

**ALEPH**

ALEPH BOOK COMPANY
An independent publishing firm
promoted by *Rupa Publications India*

Published in India in 2014 by
Aleph Book Company
7/16 Ansari Road, Daryaganj
New Delhi 110 002

ISBN: 978-93-82277-70-5

1 3 5 7 9 10 8 6 4 2

Printed and bound in India by Replika Press Pvt. Ltd.

*Dedicated*
*to the thousands of political prisoners*
*incarcerated throughout the country...*
*and to their dreams*
*of a more just society*
*that will raze the prisons to the ground*

# Contents

# Foreword

I had long feared that Arun Ferreira was going to end up on the front pages. It had been more than a decade since I'd seen him, but news of his activities would filter down through his brother, when I bumped into him on the street. Arun, he'd told me, had devoted himself to community organizing in Vidarbha, the drought-prone region in eastern Maharashtra notorious for the frequency with which its farmers took their own lives. When, in the early years of the new century, the state intensified its campaign to quell all dissent against the greed-driven model of economic development it had chosen for India, it seemed only a matter of time before apostates like Arun would become victims of its zeal.

Still, this abstract dread for the safety for my college friend did nothing to prepare me for the shock of actually seeing his photograph in the newspapers one morning in May 2007—or at least seeing an image of a squatting figure that the captions identified as Arun. Claiming that he was a 'dreaded Naxalite', the photographs showed four men on their haunches, seated at the feet of a triumphant posse of policemen in Nagpur. The heads of the captives were concealed in hoods. Clearly, the Maharashtra police had not found it necessary to pay attention to the condemnation that swept the world upon the publication of the Abu Ghraib photographs.

Over the next few days, the police invited more photographers to record the evidence of their conquests, now with their faces unshrouded. Images appeared in the papers of Arun with his hair in disarray, his eyes betraying the trauma of the ingenious forms of torture to which he had been subjected. Additional details about his alleged crimes were also leaked to the press. The police announced that he was the chief of propaganda and communications of the Maoist party, a wily operative who had an easy familiarity with sophisticated technology. They had come to this conclusion because he had a pen drive in his pocket when they arrested him.

Most often, a story about the arrest of a small band of Naxalites would have disappeared from the news cycle in a day or two. But this was different. The reporters were astonished at the fact that Arun Ferreira hailed from Bandra, the Mumbai neighbourhood that their articles routinely and unimaginatively described as 'upmarket' or 'tony'. The journalists seemed unable to understand how a man born to privilege had decided to spend his life helping people less fortunate than he was. This was something I knew a little about.

Long before soaring property prices transformed it into a neon-lit hub of chic restaurants and fashion stores, Bandra was a haven for middle-class Roman Catholics, who had laboured over the decades to create a network of schools and hospitals, orphanages and social institutions that were an admirable testament to their deep sense of Christian duty. But since the

1970s, this approach to charity had been the source of debate. The discussions had been catalysed by the publication in 1971 of Chilean philosopher Gustavo Gutiérrez's *A Theology of Liberation*.

The term 'development', Gutiérrez wrote, did not 'well express the profound aspirations' of people in underdeveloped countries 'to construct a just and fraternal society, where persons can live with dignity and be agents of their own destiny'. A more appropriate word, he suggested, was 'liberation', and went on to suggest a theoretical framework that united the quest for liberation with the Christian yearning for salvation.

As long-time residents of Bandra, Arun's family, like mine, were familiar with these discussions. One of Arun's uncles was a priest with strong views on the role the Church had in furthering the goal of social justice. By the 1980s, in the wake of the Emergency, several young Bombay Catholics who had come to an understanding of India's power dynamics as members of an organization called All-India Catholic University Federation had thrown in their lot with trade unions and human rights organizations. Arun was heir to this tradition. Not everyone chose to fight the battle outside the umbrella of the church. Shortly after Arun was finally cleared of all criminal charges, one of his neighbours on St Martin's Road, John Rodrigues, a man about the same age as us, was appointed a bishop.

When Arun dropped by to see me a few weeks after he'd obtained bail, 4 years and 8 months after being arrested, I thought he'd be contemplative, perhaps even bitter, at having been wrongly confined for so long. Instead, his wide smile and his infectious optimism filled the room. He'd brought along sketches he'd made of prison life and wanted advice on publishing them as a pamphlet. But as he began to narrate the stories behind each drawing, I knew that his experience was too vast to be confined to a mere booklet. I bullied him into expanding the scope of his text. He'd hoped to see the fruits of his labour in two months. Two years on, it's finally on the shelves.

India has very few documents of life in its horrific jails, and few as searing as this. If there's any silver lining to be found in Arun's experience, it's that he emerged seemingly unscathed. As a resurgent India throws its weight solidly behind a monochromatic vision of economic development, Arun Ferreira reminds us that diversity of opinion and debate are essential for any society to flourish. The worst thing we can do to ourselves is to imprison our imaginations.

Bombay, July 2014                                Naresh Fernandes

# 1.

# Hauladi no. 3479

Monday, 13 August 2007

> *Hi, I guess a letter from me was expected a long time ago. I have lots of things to write but have yet to familiarize myself with the rules and procedures out here. I received your postcards and money orders. With the money orders you send, I can withdraw an equivalent amount in 'coupons'. These coupons, available in denominations of 1, 2, 5 and 10, are the currency used here and I exchange them for essentials like snacks and toiletries from the canteen. I suggest you don't make too many trips to visit me. That*

*would be a waste of time and money.*

*I am presently lodged in an enclosure which has two sections containing several cells in each section. I and the persons who had been arrested with me are the only inmates kept in one of the sections. Some cells were emptied out, i.e. the inmates transferred to other places, so as to ensure that only we are kept in this section. This enclosure is infamously called the anda.*

The anda barracks are a cluster of windowless cells nestling against a high oval perimeter wall, a maximum-security zone within the high-security confines of the Nagpur Central Jail. to get to most cells from the entrance of the anda, you have to pass through five heavy iron gates, wending your way through a maze of corridors and pathways. There are several distinct compounds within the anda, each with a few cells, each cell carefully isolated from the others. Little light filters into the cells. You can't see anything outside: no greenery, no sky. There is a watchtower in the centre of the anda, and from the top, the yard must actually resemble an enormous, air-tight concrete egg. But there's a vital difference. The anda is impossible to break out of. Rather, it's designed to make inmates crack.

The anda is where the most unruly prisoners are confined, as punishment for violating disciplinary rules. The other parts of the Nagpur jail aren't quite so severe. Most prisoners are housed in barracks, with fans and a TV set. In the barracks, the daytime hours can be quite relaxed, even comfortable. But in the anda, the only ventilation you have is provided by the gate of your cell and even that doesn't afford much comfort because it opens into a covered corridor, not an open yard.

But more than the brutal, claustrophobic architecture of the anda, it's the absence of human contact that chokes you. In the anda, you spend fifteen hours or more alone in your cell. The only people you regularly see are the guards. Occasionally, you get a glimpse of the other inmates in your section. It's a situation designed to put the most robust individual under severe strain. A few weeks in the anda can cause a breakdown. The horrors of the anda are well known to prisoners in the Nagpur jail, and they would rather face the severest of beatings than be banished to this yard.

But I wasn't an ordinary prisoner. I was a 'dreaded Naxalite', a 'Maoist leader': descriptions that appeared in the newspapers the morning after my arrest on 8 May 2007. While most prisoners spend only a few weeks in the anda or in its cousin, the phasi yard—home to prisoners sentenced to death—these were the sections in which I would spend the entire 4 years and 8 months of my stay in the Nagpur jail.

3

■

It was a typical hot Nagpur summer afternoon when I was arrested at the railway station. I was waiting to meet some social activists when around fifteen men surrounded me. Some of them bundled me into a car which drove away at high speed. I was kicked and punched by them all the while. After five minutes, the car halted and I was carried to a room on the first floor of a building, which my abductors later told me was the Nagpur Police Gymkhana. From their conversations, it became evident that I had been detained by the Anti-Naxal Cell of the Nagpur police. They tied my hands with my belt and I was blindfolded, so that the officials involved in this operation would remain unidentified.

'Maar dalo saale ko. Encounter mein usse khatam karo,' they yelled, threatening to kill me in an 'encounter', or extra-judicial execution, a bluff police routinely use to scare people they've detained.

I could hear screams from the next room. Someone else was being beaten too. The blows were interspersed with questions and promises. 'Sach sach bolo to chhoda jayega' (If you tell the truth, you will be set free.) The man wasn't even given a chance to answer before I heard his next scream.

Through the day, I was flogged with belts, kicked and slapped, as they attempted to soften me up for the interrogations that were to follow. They were especially angry because no one was answering the phone at my home in Mumbai and they assumed I had given them a false address. As it turned out, my family was away on vacation. But how could I explain this to people who just wanted to beat the hell out of me?

I was afraid they'd kill me. Thus far, there was nothing official about my detention. They hadn't shown me a warrant, nor had I been taken to a police station. I feared that the police could murder me and pretend that I'd been killed in an encounter. I'd read about many situations in which the police claimed to have had no option but to open fire when suspects they were attempting to arrest had resisted. I knew that the National Human Rights Commission had noted thirty-one cases of fake encounter killings in Maharashtra alone in the previous five years. The physical torture, though painful, was relatively tame compared to this prospect.

At midnight, eleven hours after I had been detained, I was taken to a police station and informed that I had been arrested under the Unlawful Activities (Prevention) Act, 2004, which is applied to people the state brands as terrorists. I spent that night in a damp cell in the station house. My bedding was a foul-smelling black blanket, so dirty that even its dark colour could barely conceal the grime. A hole in the ground served as a urinal. It could be identified by the mass of paan stains around it and its acrid stench.

I was finally served a meal: dal, rotis and abuse. It wasn't easy to eat from a plastic bag with jaws sore from the blows I had received earlier in the day. The only solution, I learnt, was to soften the rotis by soaking them in the bag of dal. But after the horrors I had undergone, these tribulations were relatively insignificant and allowed me a brief moment to pull myself together. I managed to ignore the putrid bedding, the humid air and the ache in my body and dozed off.

Within a few hours, I was woken up for another round of questioning. The officers appeared polite at first but quickly resorted to blows in an attempt to encourage me to provide the answers they were looking for. They wanted me to disclose the location of a cache of arms and explosives or information about my supposed links with Maoists. To make me more amenable to their demands, they stretched out my body completely, using an updated version of the medieval torture technique of drawing (though there was no quartering). My arms were tied to a window grill high above the ground while two policemen stood on my outstretched thighs to keep me pinned to the floor. This was calculated to cause maximum pain without leaving visible injuries. Despite these precautions, my ears started to bleed and my jaws began to swell.

In the evening, I was forced to squat on the floor with a black hood over my head as a posse of officers posed behind me for press photographs. The next day, I would later learn, these images made the front pages of newspapers around the country. The press was told that I was the chief of communications and propaganda of the Maoist Party.

I was then produced before a magistrate. As all law students know, this measure has been introduced into legal procedure to give detenues the opportunity to complain about custodial torture—something I could establish quite easily since my face was swollen, ears bleeding and soles so sore that it was impossible to walk. But from the deliberations in court, I gathered that the police had already accounted for the injuries in the story they'd concocted about my arrest. In their version, I had fought hard with the police to try to avoid capture. They claimed they had had no option but to use force to subdue me. Strangely, none of my captors seem to have been harmed during the scuffle.

That wasn't the only surprise. In court, the police said that I'd been arrested in the company of three others—Dhanendra Bhurule, a journalist with a Marathi daily called *Deshonnati*; Naresh Bansod, the Gondia district president of the Maharashtra Andhashraddha Nirmulan Samiti (Maharashtra Superstition Eradication Committee); and Ashok Reddy, a former trade union organizer from Andhra Pradesh. The police claimed to have seized a pistol and cartridges from Ashok Reddy and a pen drive containing seditious literature from me. They said we had been meeting to hatch a plan to blow up the monument at the Deekshabhoomi in Nagpur. This is the spot where the Dalit leader Dr Bhimrao Ambedkar and more than 300,000 of his followers had converted to Buddhism in October 1956, seeking to liberate themselves from Hinduism's oppressive caste system. By manufacturing a plot to show that leftists had been planning to attack the hallowed Ambedkar shrine, the police were obviously trying to drive a wedge between Dalits and Naxalites.

But mere allegations would not be sufficient. They needed to create evidence to support their claims. The police told the court that they needed us in custody for twelve days to interrogate us. While Dhanendra Bhurule and I were kept in the Sitabuldi police station in Nagpur, the other two were taken to the Dhantoli police station. Dhantoli was the station in Nagpur where the case had been formally registered. Twice or three times a day, a constable would come to my cell to fill in the official records: 'Naam? Baap ka naam? Pata? Dhanda?' (Name? Father's name? Address? Occupation?) As he went through the routine with the man in the next cell, I realized that it was occupied by Bhurule, the journalist from Gondia, who had been accused in the same case as I was. We began to exchange a few words at mealtime.

'You want a roti? For me, one is sufficient.'

'Theek hai. Aap mera chawal lijiye,' I offered, as people from Gondia are more accustomed to rice, I thought.

'My jaws are hurting,' he said with a moan.

On the sly, we would often make sarcastic remarks about our captors, inventing nicknames for them to amuse ourselves. From our conversations, I realized that Dhanendra Bhurule was the man I had heard being beaten up in the next room the day I had been detained. He was the man the interrogators had promised to send home if he cooperated with them.

In police custody, we soon settled into a routine. Every morning, we would be transported to the Police Gymkhana for interrogation sessions that lasted late into the night. The torture techniques varied in intensity. I would be kept awake for almost 36 hours at a stretch or made to stand for long periods with my arms raised by my side, parallel to the ground. If I let them drop, a constable hit me with his lathi. At times, a group of constables would descend and force me to sit on the floor with my back against the wall. Both my legs would then be forced wide apart

7

and a cop would stand on my thighs so that I couldn't bend them. My hands were pulled up and stretched, using the window grille for leverage. All this resulted in immense pressure on my torso and groin. Sometimes my interrogators would pinch me or pull my hair or pierce the skin under my nails with pins.

The varieties of physical pain inflicted produced different reactions. The pain of the piercing, hair pulling and the like would be sharp and intense, but the body tried to and even succeeded in quickly forgetting it. Not so the forced positions and stretches. They produced a pain so all-encompassing and lasting that the body, try as it may, couldn't just get over it, and would fall into a slump. My mind however refused to submit. I could feel my anger building. 'To hell with you, I'm going to keep quiet,' I'd find myself saying. 'I'm not co-operating.' But then, I began to realize that the men assigned to torture me were not very motivated. They seemed to know that I did not have anything to tell them. They were only carrying out the instructions of their seniors to somehow get me to give my nod to the fantastic story they had concocted. As I stayed silent, they would get frustrated and they would get even more violent. Instead of me breaking down, it was my torturers who cracked as they failed to meet the expectations of their superiors. 'He's getting frustrated and he's releasing his anger by hitting me,' I would say to myself. 'I am the person who's winning and it won't be long before he gives up and just walks out. I just have to resist till that threshold point.'

■

Every forty-eight hours, we would be taken to the Government City Civil Hospital for a check-up. In 1996, the Supreme Court had made this procedure mandatory to ensure that prisoners were not tortured. But Police Sub-Inspector (PSI) Bhagel who accompanied us to the hospital made sure that the doctors did not record any wounds on paper. Bhagel would keep urging the doctors to ignore his department's excesses because we were 'dreaded terrorists'. (I have used pseudonyms for all government personnel mentioned in my account because I want to draw attention not to individuals but to the brutality of the system in which they work.)

Back at the Gymkhana, they repeatedly attempted to force us to sign a statement they had drafted confessing to our involvement with the Maoists. Through most of the interrogation sessions, I would have to squat on the ground with my hands handcuffed behind my back. After a few hours, I'd slump forward because I was so tired. But even this new position wouldn't bring any relief, so I'd try another posture. This cycle of twisting and turning would continue for hours, until I'd collapse on my back from exhaustion. For the first few days, I was not allowed a bath. The scorching Vidarbha summer had caked my clothes with the dry salt of my sweat. The dirt from squatting on the floor hadn't done much for my personal hygiene. Finally, three days after I'd been detained, I was allowed to bathe—probably because my body odour had become unbearable for my interrogators. A couple of policemen were assigned to watch me pour mugs of water over my body, lest I try to escape in the nude. It didn't bother me. By then, I had become accustomed to their omnipresent gaze. They even watched me when I was urinating.

The Dhantoli Station officer, Inspector Kanwar, was the official complainant in the case. However, because so many senior officers had descended to interrogate me, Inspector Kanwar had been reduced to being a bystander in his own lair and running errands for his superiors. Whenever a senior issued Kanwar a command in front of his constables, his ego was visibly hurt. He would sulk in a corner with a long face, waiting for the moment he could assume charge again. At the end of the day, when everyone had left, he would enter the room to talk to me. He'd come by in jeans, drunk, and slowly settle into a chair as if savouring the pleasure of regaining his throne. Venting the frustration of the insults he'd faced through the day, he would let me know in front of his constables that he was the boss and that he too knew all that was needed to be known about Maoism.

'Maoism has failed in China, it will never work here. We have people's rule!' He'd say this with a smirk when he pronounced the word 'rule'. 'Don't you bastards realize the might of the government? It will crush you easily. Why do you Naxalites kill the police? Why don't you kill the corrupt politicians?' I had once dared to reply. 'So, you want Naxalites to kill politicians?' I immediately learnt that such attempts at conversation would be injurious to my health.

At first, when he began his rants, I assumed that yet another violent interrogation session was to follow and would instinctively withdraw into myself. But after a couple of days, I realized that this was actually a form of therapy for his bruised ego. I gradually learnt to play along so that he could regain his self-esteem. This was one of my first experiences in understanding the role seniority and prestige play in the functioning of the police. (A few years on, I read that Inspector Kanwar had been suspended from duty. He had apparently beaten up some people who had come to the police station to lodge a complaint. I wasn't surprised. Someone as authoritarian as he would never stand for an ordinary citizen voicing their grievances.)

During the interrogations, the officers would be in mufti

or without their name tags. They didn't want to risk being identified or have us complain to the court about them. General complaints of torture are easily circumvented, but accusations about specific officers could be a problem. This anonymity was a violation of the Supreme Court's D.K. Basu Judgment of 1996 relating to custodial deaths. Despite the absence of stripes and badges, watching them talk to each other made it clear who was the boss within a few minutes. The presence of a senior officer would force a subordinate to stand up, straighten their back and address him as 'Sir'.

In my early days of police custody, I began to understand what interrogation, taaba (custody) and pee-cee-aar meant. In legal terminology, Police Custodial Remand or PCR refers to a situation in which the police have authority over the accused person, a condition that is different from judicial custody, in which the accused person is lodged in jail on behalf of the court, awaiting trial. But in police usage, it is a verb form of the brutal interrogation to which detenues are subjected: 'Uska pee-cee-aar kiya,' policemen would say, or 'Hum tera pee-cee-aar kara denge.' During pee-cee-aar, when one is lodged in a police lock-up, one's constitutionally guaranteed rights are always under threat. The right to silence, for one, is guaranteed in the Indian Constitution under Article 20(3). However, every time I—perhaps naively—sought refuge in this fundamental right, it would only entail more torture.

Among my more sadistic interrogators was Abhishek Kapur, the Deputy Commissioner of Police in charge of Crime for Nagpur. He was a strapping young IPS officer, always striving for the favour of his seniors. Terrorist bashing would definitely get him a few more credits. While interrogating me, he would make it a point to make me squat on the ground handcuffed, while he sat on a chair in front of me. His ego would swell every time he looked down at me and asserted that he was from Delhi's prestigious St. Stephen's College, a statement intended to demonstrate that he was a class apart from the other officers. But if I chose to remain silent to his questions, he would kick my jaw with his boots. I came to realize that I had been strategically placed so that he could use minimum effort to do so.

From the chatter of the police constables, I learnt that in 2006 Abhishek Kapur had been in charge of the zone in Nagpur where the agitation against the Khairlanji killings had started. Indora Basti is the biggest Dalit settlement in Nagpur, famous for its militant politics. When the news spread of how four members of the lower-caste Bhotmange family had been paraded naked and then lynched by a mob of upper-caste villagers in Khairlanji village in Bhandara district, Indora was the first community to erupt in anger. Dalit youth gathered at Indora Chowk, burning tyres. The police responded with a lathi charge and arrested some activists. Lower-level police staff believed that the incompetent handling of these protests had caused the agitation to spread through Nagpur and then across Maharashtra. Senior officers, on the other hand, blamed Maoists for organizing the agitation. I was trapped by their spurious theory. Abhishek Kapur had a compelling reason to claim that he'd arrested four Maoists in the city within a year of the agitation.

But it wasn't only officers of the Nagpur police who were interrogating me. I gathered that I was being questioned, among others, by officers from the Anti-Naxal Cell, the Anti-Terrorism Squad, the Intelligence Bureau and even the Special Intelligence Bureau of Andhra Pradesh. They would come in batches of two to three. Their seniors would stay in the background, designating the work of interrogation to their juniors. The 'good cop-bad cop' routine was one of their regular tricks. They also tried another tactic: they'd tell me that the people they'd arrested along with me had confessed to their involvement with the Maoists, so it was pointless for me to attempt to resist. When this proved unproductive, they'd revert to their routine of hammering me and stretching out my limbs.

This went on for ten days. When all their tactics failed, the police got the court to allow them to subject Ashok Reddy and me to the scientifically dubious practice of narco-analysis, lie detectors and brain-mapping tests. They hoped to use the results of these tests to conjure up evidence for their allegations.

We did not consent to these tests. So PSI Bhagel repeatedly used threats and sleight of hand to try to make me sign a paper stating that 'as I was telling the truth, I consent to such tests'. A letter of consent is now ethically and medically mandatory, but could, in 2007, be waived by an order of the court.

Even before detenues can undergo narco-analysis, they are put through a series of medical tests, ostensibly to ascertain whether they are fit enough to withstand these procedures. In reality, the tests determine the prisoner's levels of resistance and help the authorities calculate how much of the drug, sodium pentothal, can be administered without the subject collapsing. These preliminary tests were conducted on us in the city's civil hospital. Preparations got underway to transport us to the State Forensic Science Lab in Mumbai.

But before that, we were produced before the magistrate. As Section 167 of the Code of Criminal Procedure permits the magistrate to authorize the detention of the accused in police custody for a term not exceeding fifteen days in the whole, the police could not obtain additional custody in the same case. (After 2008, an amendment in the Unlawful Activities Prevention Act has increased the term to thirty days.) So the police registered new cases: I was charged with being a member of an unlawful assembly, committing an unlawful act, conspiring to do a terrorist act and being a member of an organization that had committed a terrorist act. All these related to their accusation that we had assembled at Deekshabhoomi to hatch a criminal conspiracy as members of the Communist Party of India (Maoist), which has been banned since 2009.

The CPI (Maoist) represents the most radical strand within the 90-year-old Indian Communist movement. The Communist Party of India had been founded in 1925, inspired by the success of the Russian Bolshevik Revolution. During British rule, the CPI had organized millions of industrial workers and, not surprisingly, faced considerable repression. Hundreds of CPI members were arrested and many of them were charged in conspiracy cases. However after the British rule, the party took to the parliamentary path and even formed a state level government in Kerala in 1957. Differences within the party on relations with China and other matters led to a split. This resulted in the formation of the Communist Party of India (Marxist) in 1964. The new party also continued to engage in parliamentary politics. However, radicals believed that this engagement in parliamentary politics constituted an unacceptable collaboration with an oppressive state and an abandonment of the revolutionary struggle. After a peasant uprising in the Naxalbari village of West Bengal in 1967, these groups coalesced. The CPI (Maoist), formed in 2004, is a further ideological and organizational consolidation of this revolutionary tendency. Because of the site of the conflict to which they trace their origins, Indian Maoists are also referred to as Naxalbadis or Naxalites.

More than forty years after the Naxalbari revolt, the Naxalite movement has emerged as a formidable socio-political, armed force in mobilising the most oppressed Indians who have been left untouched by development. The Maoists seek to overthrow the state and replace it with a more democratic one. As a result, the government banned the CPI (Maoist) as a terrorist organisation under the Unlawful Activities (Prevention) Act and has sought to criminalize any sympathy for the movement.

In my case, merely suggesting that I held radical beliefs was sufficient cause for the state to invoke criminal charges. If convicted, I would be imprisoned for life. That day, after the court hearing, we were transferred to judicial custody.

■

On 20 May 2007, I stooped to enter the low, narrow door of Nagpur Central Prison, which would be my home for the next fifty-four months. It had been twelve days since I'd been arrested. In keeping with procedure, first-time prisoners are presented before the gate officer. Tradition, and perhaps training, demands that even the most mild-mannered gate officer be at his aggressive best while dealing with new entrants, who, in jail slang, are called naya aamad. It's one of many Urdu words commonly used in prison, remnants of the British era. Like all other isolated communities, the prison is frozen in time. I realized that it is the gate officer's job to give the newcomer a crash course in meekness and mindless subservience. The lathi at his side serves as a teaching aid.

The gate officer is programmed to verbally abuse the new prisoner at the slightest sign that he is straying from total submission. Standing too close to the gate officer's desk or too far, too straight or too bent, hands behind or hands in front all qualify as unacceptable behaviour.

The officer is supposed to enquire whether the new prisoner has suffered injuries due to torture in police custody and, if so, record his statement. In my case, I had a bleeding ear, swollen jaws and sore feet. (In reality, the officer threatens anyone trying to make a complaint. By custom, all injuries are recorded as having existed before the prisoner was arrested.) A strip search followed, standard protocol for new entrants to the prison. I was stripped to my underwear and ordered to squat in a line with the other new entrants, awaiting my turn with the man in charge of the searches, who was known as the jhadati-amaldar. Every crevice of our bodies was examined and our every belonging scrutinized before being thrown on the dirty roadway for us to pick up. Grave hazards like packets of biscuits and beedis were pocketed by the staff.

If the prisoner's wait at the gate coincides with the entry or exit of one of the senior jail officials, he is privileged to witness a ceremony of colonial vintage. Senior jailers and superintendents cannot be expected to bend low to enter through the small door, so the main gate is swung open to allow the sahibs to walk through, heads held high. When the dignitaries are sighted at a distance, the gate guard issues a yelp of caution: 'ALL HUP!' All staff spring to attention and all lower life-forms are swept into corners out of sight, or forced to squat on their haunches.

Most naya aamads are then taken to the 'after barrack', where they spend a night or two before being assigned to a permanent barrack, or 'fixed barrack'. This waiting period allows the jail staff, convict warders, in-house extortionist gangs and other sharks to assess what monetary and other benefits they can extract from their latest prey. Middle-class entrants and more affluent detenues are easy targets. They are softened up with stories of the horrors of prison life and not-so-veiled threats. Younger men are targeted for free labour and for use as sex objects. Contacts are made and deals are struck to ensure better treatment when the new prisoners are moved to the fixed barracks.

Next is the mulaiza or check-in process. A convict warder or jailer lectures new prisoners about the value of prison discipline. The identifying marks of each new inmate are noted and he is weighed, measured and examined by a doctor and psychologist before being presented before a phalanx of prison divinities, led by the superintendent. A Body Ticket is presented to each prisoner, listing his prisoner number and the offences registered against him. These offences form the basis of how he will be classified and, to some extent, how he will be treated in jail. Convicts (kaidis) and undertrials (havalathis, commonly pronounced as hauladi) are counted separately. I was now hauladi number 3479 of 2007.

Even though the law states an accused person is innocent until proven guilty, such niceties lack meaning behind prison walls. The allegations of the police are sufficient evidence for the jail authorities to punish even those awaiting trial. Alleged rapists are routinely targeted by officers at the time of entry itself. One particularly macho type would force rape accused to crawl in the afternoon sun from the gate to the barracks—an exercise that would quickly produce thick blisters on the arms and knees. In the barracks they would be set upon enthusiastically by other prisoners with the encouragement of the staff. The most righteous ones leading the attacks were often themselves rape accused or convicts. Such were some of the ironies of the prison 'justice' system.

Those implicated in murder cases are compelled to wear the convict prisoner uniform and are consigned to special 'murder barracks'. People accused of terrorism are invariably sent to places such as the anda barrack and many jail superintendents personally preside over their beatings as a sign of their patriotism.

Before the mulaiza, procedure requires the new entrant to be bathed. However, shortages of soap and water often prevent the diligent observance of these rules. Instead, most naya aamads are rushed through the rough-and-ready hands of the nai kamaan (literally, the Barber Command), one of the work groups to which prisoners could be assigned later. Some colonial-era jail bureaucrat with a fiendish yearning for military discipline or a wicked sense of humour probably established the tradition of calling each work-team a kamaan (or command).

The naya aamad's next stop is the Badi Gol, the area in Nagpur jail that houses prisoners awaiting trial. That, theoretically, is where I should have been headed. But in my case, the procedures were cut short. The police report was sufficient for exceptions to be made to the elaborate procedures. I was hurriedly put into the anda barrack, given a thick white cotton prison uniform and after a quick meal of besan and chewy rotis at 4 p.m. was on my way to Mumbai by train, along with Ashok Reddy, to undergo narco-analysis.

■

Just before boarding the train, Ashok and I were given new sets of clothes, our first change in twelve days. We later learnt that our lawyers had asked a friendly police officer to help. I was also given an old pair of rubber slippers. The cops had misplaced my sandals immediately after my arrest and during the days in custody or travelling to court, the gymkhana or the hospital, I had been walking barefoot. The baking Nagpur summer heat had made the tar roads sizzle, so I'd have to run from the station to the van.

About a dozen brawny policemen wielding Kalashnikovs were designated to accompany us on our journey. To be doubly sure that nothing went wrong, we were kept handcuffed to our berths throughout the 15-hour journey to Mumbai.

Thus far, I had not been allowed to speak with Ashok, even though he had been implicated along with me. We would occasionally glance sympathetically at each other whenever we were seated together in the courtroom or at the civil hospital during our mandatory examinations. This silence was also enforced on the train journey to Mumbai, probably to prevent us from exchanging ideas on how to tackle our interrogators. The first time I had a chance to talk to Ashok was when we reached Azad Maidan police station, near Mumbai's Chhatrapati Shivaji Terminus. We were to spend a night here before being taken for our interrogation. The Nagpur police, led by Kanwar, had managed to secure a separate cell for the two of us. This had involved fierce arguments with the Mumbai cops and drawing on the influence of his seniors. However, seeing us conversing in the lock-up, they soon realized their blunder and we were shifted out within an hour. We were then kept in a police staff room of the Azad Maidan police station under Kanwar's direct supervision. They feared our conversations would affect the results of the narco-analysis tests that were to be conducted the next day.

The day after we arrived, we were shifted to the Arthur Road Prison in Jacob Circle. Learning that I had been brought to Mumbai, my mother, brother and sister attempted to visit me in the prison. They were denied permission, so they stood

19

outside the gate for hours, hoping to catch a glimpse of me in transit. It was not to be. But our time in Arthur Road wasn't without its benefits. Many inmates there gave us a briefing on the procedures of narco-analysis and generously gave us pointers on how to muddy the results, though none of their strategies were of any use because they didn't seem to be logical. Nonetheless, this was an example of the respect with which ordinary prisoners normally treat detenues accused of terrorism, considering the political and selfless nature of their alleged crimes.

On 22 May, I was transported to an operation theatre at the J.J. Hospital, a government institution with backup facilities for surgery. This was essential because sodium pentothal, the drug used in narco-analysis, can cause the heart to slow down— fatally. The psychologist asked me to sign some papers, which I did only after noting my protest and the compulsion of the court order on every page.

The drug was administered like a drip, at a controlled pace, so that I would remain in a trance for an extended time. Although the police were not permitted to enter the room, the forensic experts used the drug with police-like efficiency, with total disregard for medical ethics or my health. The police had prepared a list of questions for the psychologist to ask. As the so-called truth serum dripped into my body, the psychologist launched into her warm-up questions. The conversation was video recorded and, years later, I watched myself on the table: 'What is your name?', 'How old are you?' and 'What's your birthday?', 'Where do you stay?'

Soon the drug was taking over. I grew drowsy and my speech started getting slurry. 'I'm feeling sleepy,' I'd often reply, so the questions asked started getting more serious: 'Do you know of the CPI (Maoist)?'

'Yes.'

'Where do they keep their arms?'

'Don't know.'

'Have you used some kind of arms, at least for self-protection?'

'No.'

'Are you aware of any doctors or hospitals that provide services to the Maoist group?'

'No.'

'Are you aware of any safe houses in Nagpur where their leaders come and stay?'

'No... I don't know much about Nagpur.'

So, you have any idea of their Mumbai safe houses?'

'No.'

The questioning went on for a little less than an hour. As my tongue got increasingly heavier, my speech incoherent and no tangible results were forthcoming, the psychologist began getting desperate. From questions regarding my alleged association with Maoists, she moved to my beliefs.

'In all these struggles you have undertaken, what is the most extreme step you have taken?'

'I have taken ... (slur)... morchas and rallies...'

'Have you and your organization been involved in violence?'

'(slur) ...no... not much.'

'Not much?!'

'... There has been (slur)... no need to do so...'

'But if the need arose would you do so?'

'... (slur) ...Yes.'

'So you have no problem with using violence for fighting for the rights of people?'

'(slur) … Yes.'

'Have you utilized violence?'

'No…(slur)'

'Absolutely not?'

'No…'

There it was. They finally got the proof they needed. By my own confession, my intentions were criminal and violent. The narco was successful and she concluded: 'Arun, you can sleep now.'

After I woke, I remembered some of the questions I'd been asked. It was like recollecting a dream: I didn't remember all the details, but I hadn't forgotten the highlights.

A day later, I was taken to the Forensic Science Laboratory at Kalina for a polygraph test—popularly known as a lie-detector test—which recorded several physiological parameters such as blood pressure, pulse and respiration, while I was made to answer a series of questions. These physiological indices were measured by sensors placed on my fingertips, palms and strapped to my chest. The technology works on the assumption that deceptive answers produce heightened physiological responses. But the questions they asked were ridiculous. 'Do you know Javed, Sachin and Jyoti?' Answering in the affirmative would mean that I knew someone named Javed, Sachin or Jyoti who was a Maoist.

The brain mapping tests were similar. I was taken to a soundproof room similar to a recording studio. Thirty-two electrodes were attached to my scalp and I was made to listen to a series of statements on headphones, many regarding my involvement in the alleged offences. The electrodes would record my responses to these propositions, map the electrical changes in my brain and allegedly determine whether I had any 'experiential knowledge' of the event to calculate the truthfulness of my claims. When I was finally given the report after several months, I learnt that this purportedly scientific test inferred that I had repeatedly lied, even about my name and being married:

**Probe:** My name is Arun Ferreira—Nil experiential knowledge.

**Probe:** I am married—Nil experiential knowledge.

These tests were conducted on me at a time that courts dared not doubt their scientific validity. It was only three years later, in May 2010, that a three-judge bench of the Supreme Court headed by the Chief Justice held that the use of narco-analysis, brain-mapping and polygraph tests without the consent of the subject was unconstitutional and a violation of the right to privacy.

After almost a week in my hometown, I was brought back to the Nagpur prison by road. The police, meanwhile, prepared themselves to charge me with more cases so that they could continue to hold me in custody and pee-cee-aar for some more time.

23

■

From 28 May to 14 June 2007, I was slapped with five more cases relating to Naxalite violence in Gondia, a district about 150 kilometres from Nagpur. Gondia and especially Gadchiroli, the other district lying at the extreme end of Maharashtra, are areas of intense Maoist activity. In almost all of Gadchiroli and parts of Gondia, armed Naxal squads have fought the police and paramilitary forces with support from the local tribals and peasants. This is in keeping with the Maoist strategy to establish revolutionary centres in rural areas in the hope of eventually growing to seize power throughout the country. It is no coincidence that these districts are also among the poorest areas in Maharashtra. In 2011, Gadchiroli had the lowest ranking on the state's Human Development Index.

The five new cases allowed the police to get me back into their custody for another twenty-three days, till 19 June. I was shifted to Amgaon, a police station in the interiors of Gondia, where I was subjected to more sleep deprivation, harassment and interrogation. This time though, I was fortunate to get away relatively lightly. But my co-accused were not so lucky. The police, under the direct supervision of the sub-divisional police officer, a man named Korate, injected petrol into the rectums of two of them. A couple of staff lifted their legs while an inspector infiltrated the 20 ml of petrol into their bodies. The vapours of gasoline burned the intestine linings, which resulted in agonizing days of anal bleeding, blood clots and continuous belching. I wonder how Korate knew that exactly 20 ml of petrol would cause such enormous pain yet not kill. Such knowledge could only have been acquired by some sort of training. Ashok Reddy did manage to complain to the court about this. However the state-appointed doctor, obviously a friend of Korate's, diagnosed Ashok's condition as piles and exonerated the officer and his accomplices.

I was, for reasons best known to them, protected from such treatment. The police would come by to interrogate me every couple of days—whenever they got a list of questions from a superior. When I didn't reply to their first question, they never got further down the list, and that's where the torture would start.

'Arre, Bajirao ko bulao,' the inspector would call.

A narrow belt attached to a wooden handle would be

brought in by a constable—an implement that policemen across Maharashtra fondly call 'Bajirao'. It takes its name from Peshwa Baji Rao, a lieutenant of Shahu Maharaj, a ruler who is credited with greatly expanding the Maratha Empire. Maharashtra's police personnel, largely dominated by the Maratha caste, find this instrument similarly trustworthy. The Bajirao belt was deployed carefully, only on the palms or soles of the feet. When whipped, the cluster of nerves at the heel pad causes enormous pain but displays no external injuries, so I wouldn't have any proof if I tried to complain to a magistrate. However, doctors know that such foot whipping can cause permanent nerve damage. It reduces the elasticity of the heel pad causing agonizing aches, especially on cold nights, for years afterwards. Such torture, though not so visible to the naked eye, leads to irreversible harm to the body.

Once in a while, often due to the inexperience or over enthusiasm of the torturer, this permanent damage extends to death. No wonder Maharashtra still retains its privileged position of having the highest number of custodial deaths in India. It recorded 22 in 2011, way ahead of Gujarat, which came next with 7 deaths. Invariably, the government's National Crime Records Bureau (NCRB) attributes these deaths to natural causes or to suicide. People like Korate and his seniors are never held responsible.

■

After 23 days and nights in the Gondia lock-up, we were brought back to Nagpur jail. For the first time in the month-and-a-half since my arrest, my family was allowed to meet me. My father and brother in Mumbai had contacted my lawyer, who had arranged for them to meet me at the court. I heard about their side of hell. They told me about their shock at seeing my name and photograph in the papers, and of reading the police descriptions of the violence in which I had allegedly been involved. At first, my brother and sister had desperately tried to hide the news from my ageing parents, but weren't able to do so for very long. They told me that soon after hearing of my arrest, my wife, a lecturer in a Mumbai college, had fallen off a motorcycle and bruised her face badly. I heard how the police had searched our home, seizing books and dismantling our computer. They also seized my wife's sociology books and my 2-year-old son's CDs of nursery rhymes as 'incriminating' evidence. On the sly, the police had pocketed digital watches and pens.

Most of the time that day at court went in getting my father and brother to believe that I hadn't committed the blasts, murders and other violent crimes of which I'd been accused and which they'd read about in the media. The reports had parroted the police line, with little regard for the truth. For instance, the *Mumbai Mirror* had reported on 11 May: '…Nagpur police which carried out a search at Ferreira's residence on Wednesday …maintains that he is a high-ranking leader of the banned organization Communist Party of India (Maoist) and that in his capacity as chief of propaganda for the ultra-left outfit, he was responsible for spreading violence.'

The little time I had with my family in court was insufficient to clarify all their doubts. The next 4 years and 8 months would also prove insufficient.

My brother told me that a group of college friends and well-wishers in Mumbai had got together to campaign for my release. Well-attended meetings were being organized, which used my case to prove that narco-analysis was just another form of torture. But their efforts were crushed when the Nagpur city Police Commissioner threatened to arrest my friends if they attempted to meet me in jail. My family had approached many government bodies such as the State Minorities Commission, State Home Department and high-ranking police officers. However, other than empty promises to look into the matter, they had nothing to offer.

Soon, my life acquired a predictable pattern. The police would implicate me in new cases, obtain custody to interrogate me, inflict terrible torture on me, fail to extract a confession, return me to jail, only to involve me in yet another case. After two months, I had six cases registered against me. It was only when the police finally filed charge sheets, laying out evidence for why I should be prosecuted, that I had a new routine. It involved making weekly or sometimes daily trips to court to wait for the cases to be heard. The initial shock dissipated and I started getting accustomed to the luxury of contemplating the myriad rhythms of prison life.

# 2.

# The Anda

Saturday, 8 September 2007

*Legally I have been implicated in six cases till now. I don't think this number will increase. However, due to the arrest of two more political dissenters [Sridhar Srinivasan and Vernon Gonsalves, both in their mid-fifties] in Mumbai who the state now regularly refers to as Maoists, my name has once again begun to appear in the newspapers. Guess this is going to be a regular feature; I might as well start getting accustomed to it.*

*Your letter mentions how this year has taken a heavy toll*

*on the entire family. This is not far from the truth. However, remember the strong get through difficulties, victorious and even stronger. It is the weak who collapse and give up hope. I don't think you have taught me to be the latter. Keep writing, your letters help.*

Letters to my family were not only a medium for communication but also a pretext for mutual consolation. On the arrival of my messages, my wife would come to Bandra almost immediately to meet with Mom and Dad. My elder brother and sister who lived nearby would drop by too and my letter would invariably result in a family discussion. The children playing in the adjoining room were oblivious to the problems the family was facing.

Bandra, a former suburb of Mumbai, but now part of the expanding city, was the place of my birth and where I grew up. As a schoolboy, my worldview was limited by the boundaries of this suburb, a righteous Christian upbringing and the impractical, lofty aspirations of a typical middle-class family. I had my first brush with social activism as a student at Mumbai's St. Xavier's College in the early 1990s. I'd organized camps in villages and welfare projects for the underprivileged. Through such camps I became exposed to the harsh realities of India and the limitations of charity. I clearly recollect an encounter at a camp in Talasari in Thane district in 1991 where we spent our days enthusiastically building a road for the villagers. In the evenings, we would chat with the residents or have cultural performances for their entertainment and education. When I visited a house in the Dalit pada (hamlet), one resident asked me why we were holding the camp. I proudly told him it was to build a road so that they could reach the market more easily. He told me that the location of the road we were constructing would allow only the sarpanch and other members of upper-caste families to get to the market. The majority of the villagers, especially the poor and the Dalits, would still use the old kuccha road. I was unintentionally deepening an already existing social division.

Indian society, I realized that day, was fractured by class and caste and riddled with innumerable contradictions. Power vested in the economic and social elite, and the benefits of development flowed disproportionately to them. Unless these structures were changed, charity would be meaningless.

The communal riots of 1992-1993 that followed the destruction of the Babri Masjid in Ayodhya really shook me up. The riots had caused thousands of Muslims to be displaced in their own city. I was in my final year of college, soon to become a Maths graduate. A group of us from St. Xavier's decided to work with a housing rights organization that was running relief camps for Muslims. The callousness of the state, which allowed the Shiv Sena to conduct this pogrom unimpeded, could not have been on better display. The Shiv Sena and other Hindu fundamentalist mobs acquired voter lists so that they could systematically target Muslims, while the police threatened to fire on any sign of resistance from the victims. Thousands of Muslim houses were burnt and the residents were shifted to relief camps and community centres. In such a surcharged atmosphere, to speak of fighting the oppressors would be seen as an act of communal violence. The least we could do was to collect clothes and funds to help the victims put their lives back together.

Kartik Pannalal, a former student of my college, was a friend during these times. He had left his family's diamond business to work to build a just society. He regularly visited St. Xavier's to organize the college canteen workers who were agitating for their rights, including the right to unionize. He helped them stage several strikes and we tried to get the students to support them. I'd spent long days in college involving myself in the lives of the workers, having heated discussions with student union leaders and then in the evening, chatting with the workers and discussing working-class issues over endless cups of chai.

Through Kartik, I came to realize that there were many more like us—organizations and movements across the country and around the world that were working with the same ideals. I joined one such revolutionary student organization, the Vidyarthi Pragati Sanghatana (VPS), which had units in several colleges. It had student committees in Mumbai, Nagpur, Nashik and Chandrapur and also a state-level committee. The VPS was a member of a national organization called the All India Revolutionary Students' Federation. The activities of the VPS centred on the struggle for a democratic, scientific and egalitarian educational system. But education, like all other aspects of society, could not be transformed in isolation. Hence, we would strive to build and support other struggles aiming at the radical transformation of class and caste society.

Even though the Western world was tom-tomming its so-called victory over Marxism as the Soviet Union disintegrated, I was getting attracted to the ideology. Stories of the French Revolution as well as the Russian and Chinese revolutions impressed on me the true potential of the oppressed to effect social change. Society needed qualitative leaps or revolutions to bring about change and the present world order wasn't the end of history. Unfortunately, my co-traveller on these intellectual journeys, Kartik, died in a road accident in Delhi in June 1997. He was on his way back from a fact-finding enquiry into military excesses in the Kashmir valley. He was only 29. Society had lost a committed civil-liberties activist and I, a great friend.

While in the VPS, I had the opportunity to meet with youth from diverse backgrounds, especially from the working class and lower castes. Many of them inspired me with their talent and zeal to change society. The more oppressed they were, the greater their commitment. We organized many struggles against fee-hikes and against a proposed University Bill that would do away with elections to student unions and select representatives based on academic merit. But the Bill was enacted in 1994, and landed a major blow to student politics in Mumbai. Student unions became student councils and were deprived of any autonomy.

The VPS also managed to highlight the corruption of Dr S. D. Karnik, the pro vice-chancellor of the Bombay University, and successfully organized students to demand his ouster in 1995. We organized annual 'go-to-the-villages' campaigns across western India to help the dispossessed assert their rights. In the Nashik campaign, we supplemented the efforts of tribals who were organizing against the atrocities of the Forest Department. In Dabhol, we took part in the struggle of villagers who were resisting the Enron power project. In Umergaon, Gujarat, it was the fisherfolk who were protesting their imminent displacement by a gigantic, upcoming port.

Looking at all these struggles up close made me aware of the true potential of peoples' movements as agencies of change. Real change meant questioning the unequal relations of power and organizing the people to claim their rights themselves. These struggles showed me how the state was the principal tool of oppression. The state institutionalized oppression. The violence it perpetrated crushed any challenge. As a result, many sincere peoples' movements such as the Naxalite and secessionist movements in Kashmir and the Northeast had to evolve militantly in order to survive. In such a situation, I could not condemn the militancy of these groups. It had a historical and political context.

After college, I continued for a couple of years in the student movement and later, I joined the Naujawan Bharat Sabha, a youth organization that got its name from a body founded in 1926 by the revolutionary freedom fighter Shaheed Bhagat Singh. In the late 1990s, the Naujawan Bharat Sabha was involved in the struggles of Mumbai slum dwellers protesting the demolitions of their homes. At that time, the city was witnessing a series of slum demolitions as a result of the Slum Rehabilitation Scheme announced by the newly elected Shiv Sena government. It allowed developers to build luxury towers on slum land. The timing of this scheme coincided with a spike in property prices, so construction companies were eager to get to work as soon as possible. Slum dwellers took to the streets. We helped mobilize them and organized agitations along with many other groups. I stayed in these bastis for weeks. Organizing struggles, I realized, was not only compelling but also absorbing.

This was also the time when globalization began showing its ugly face and people all over the world began to take to the streets. The Seattle movement in 1999 and the militant Genoa mobilizations in 2001 against the World Trade Organization and G-8 summits inspired us. Many of us in the city and in Maharashtra were keen on building similar, broad anti-capitalist peoples' movements. To do this, organizations and activists across the state had to be contacted and consulted. I involved myself in this task.

After the World Trade Center attack in New York in 2001,

however, there was a change in the way peoples' movements came to be perceived. The so-called 'War Against Terror' made security a key aspect of state policy. In India, special laws were promulgated to squash inconvenient truths. Organizations were banned, opinions were criminalized and social movements were branded as terrorist. Those who supported the right to self-determination of Kashmiris or of the peoples of the Northeast were termed anti-national. Muslims who battled against Hindutva were termed jihadis. Those of us Marxists who worked to organize tribals or the oppressed were easily labelled as left-wing extremists. The VPS, Naujawan Bharat Sabha and other organizations I had worked with were systematically targeted. Just as it had in colonial times, the Naujawan Bharat Sabha again faced a ban.

In 2005, Prime Minister Manmohan Singh declared that Maoists were 'India's greatest internal security threat'. Some were 'encountered' or 'disappeared', while others were arrested. In places like Chhattisgarh, Jharkhand or Vidarbha in Maharashtra, left-leaning political organizations were branded as Maoist and dealt with accordingly. In the months before my detention, many Dalit activists in Nagpur had been arrested on the charges of radicalizing the Ambedkarite movement by infusing it with the politics of Naxalism. Some of them had previously been associated with the Nagpur unit of the VPS. All this meant that I wasn't entirely unprepared to be arrested.

Still, even though I'd contemplated this hypothetical situation, I wasn't completely prepared to become a target of these excesses myself—to be arrested, tortured, implicated in false cases with fabricated evidence and to be locked away in prison for several years.

**8 September 2007 (Contd.)**

*The old TIME magazines you sent were great. I also received the sweaters you had sent. The other clothes were loose. I have probably lost weight during police custody. I now eat dinner at 6.30 p.m. and I am off to sleep by 8 p.m.—can't afford to allow the food to get any colder. My court visits continue. However since many of the dates overlap, the frequency of these trips has reduced. I have run short of some good reading material. Try sending me some by post or whenever someone comes next.*

My letters from prison had to pass through various layers of officialdom before they finally reached the post box. The guards would first make an entry in their register before sending the letter to the jailer in charge of the barrack. An inquisitive guard would always comment on its contents, especially if the letter was in English, I suspect to prove his own command over the language. The mention of an inmate in my letter could very well be the next topic of gossip or the cause of the next argument, so I had to be careful. The jailer would then censor the letter. Material that criticized the administration was obviously discouraged. We would be summoned and lectured on how such writing would incite prison disrespect and indiscipline. Disparaging remarks about the jailer could not even be contemplated. In our high-profile case, photocopies of our letters were filed away, to be shown periodically to the Anti-Naxal Department of the police. Once, the jailer insisted I remove criticism of the prime minister from a letter. 'Rule 12 of the Prison Manual states that "political matters are not to be discharged at interviews" and in letters,' he asserted. Hence, comments in letters had to be framed with

35

some deliberation. I had to stick to the facts as far as possible. But how could I hide my emotions? That is what my family wanted to hear. Initially, I used cryptic terminology, but as the years passed by and I grew familiar with the system, I began to disregard the snooping eyes.

The two-star jailer of the anda was Nagdev Pawar. His seniority in the department should have given him the post of a three-star, or senior jailer, but he had once been suspended because he'd been accused of beating an inmate to death. This, I found out, was a regular practice in the prison department. Almost all officers had been accused of misdeeds at some point in their careers. Corruption and negligence in duty were the most common charges. Allegations such as torture and beatings would rarely result in an officer being suspended unless this had led to the death of a prisoner. Even if he was suspended, it barely seemed to matter. The case would continue for years and, after being acquitted, the officer would be reinstated with full back-pay. Moreover, because of a shortage of jail staff, the administration would often summon staff back to duty even during their period of suspension.

Nagdev Pawar's de facto seniority in the Nagpur prison gave him additional responsibilities and also immunity. He'd visit the anda only before the superintendent's weekly round. Strolling in, with his pants pulled up almost to his chest, he would casually enquire if we had any requests or complaints. He had a very strange way of dealing with our grievances. Whenever we complained of the poor food or the fact that the same vegetables were served at every meal for days on end, he'd reply that he had to cope with the same situation in his sarkari quarters. His experience from all his years of dealing with inmates had obviously taught him that since he couldn't solve our problems, he'd be better off claiming to share them. Either this was true, or he was actually skimming off our prison rations.

As the four of us co-accused (or numberkaari, in jail terminology) were all socially aware, we were quick to respond and react to the absurdities and injustices that were commonplace in the prison system. This is what we all had done earlier and it united us behind bars. One of our first struggles with Nagdev Pawar and the prison administration was to obtain a copy of the Prison Manual, which determined every detail of how life should be conducted in jail. At first, the administration ignored our plea and later claimed that they didn't actually possess a copy. This was ridiculous, the Prison Manual was their rule book after all. Like the Penal Code and Criminal Procedure, rules for prison administration were first codified by the British in the latter part of the nineteenth century. The Prisons Act of 1894, adopted to keep unruly natives under control, remains the guiding protocol for prison administration long after 1947. After the Constitution came into effect in 1950, the administration of prisons became the responsibility of state governments. In the years that followed, the Maharashtra government enacted numerous new prison rules. These, along with the Indian Prisons Act, are collectively known as the Maharashtra Prison Manual. British jail officials were known to have denied prisoners any access to the Prison Manual. Nagdev Pawar and Co. seemed to want to continue this colonial legacy by denying us a copy of the rule book.

■

Life in the anda makes one crave for news of the outside. There was one particular spot in the anda where we could view a few leaves of the trees beyond the wall. Instinctively, that became the spot where the four of us numberkaari gathered to chat before bandi—just before sunset—when all the barracks were locked for the night. In the absence of an alternative, frequently narrated stories became a source of great amusement. We would try to start a conversation with Chandu of the danda kamaan who came to clean the toilets, or members of the jhadu kamaan who came to fill water in our peepas—the 15-litre tin cans in our cells—when the regular supply failed. The jhadu kamaan, if offered a beedi, would chat till they were exhausted. To encourage these precious snatches of conversation, we began purchasing smokes from the prison canteen.

Lean and middle-aged Chandu would, every morning after the opening of bandi, waddle in with a garbage pail in one hand and a broom in the other to empty the jhootan, the leftovers. He would bring life into the anda every morning with his rustic chatter, filling us with news of barrack life the night before. On his evening trips, just before bandi, he would be much more relaxed and had longer to chat, as his danda kamaan team were the last to be locked up after they'd cleaned the prison-yard toilets. Chandu was from a village in Nagpur district and had been convicted for a murder he had committed on behalf of a friend. Though the friend was acquitted, Chandu was jailed for life. He was the first to educate us about various jail procedures and how to get around the most cumbersome of these. Through him, we were able to communicate with the handful of other prisoners accused of being Naxalites and who were also clients of my lawyer.

Javed Gulam Hussein, a fellow inmate of the anda, had another method of breaking the monotony. He was a Pakistani in his late forties convicted in a bomb blast case in Mumbai in

1998. The police had claimed that he was part of the group that set off five bombs on the railway tracks that year. Although no lives were lost in the explosions, the trial court sentenced him to 'double life', with no pardon whatsoever—two life sentences that were to run consecutively. He could stay in for more than 70 years. Initially, Javed's dark, sunken eyes, Pathan physique and long beard terrified me. But I would later learn that this Rawalpindi native was harmless and homesick most of the time. He would regularly express the deepest of his emotions in beautiful Urdu shayiri.

Javed had come to tour Mumbai in his youth and was arrested from a lodge in 1998 just after the blasts. With no contact with his family, his cravings for the outside world were chronic. Almost every other day, he would complain that he had developed an allergic rash and needed to be immediately taken to the prison hospital for treatment. Often, these complaints flared up into arguments with the guards. However, if he was allowed the trip to the prison hospital, he would be back a different man. He'd be calmer. Meeting the doctor or getting medication was irrelevant. Making human contact was what mattered.

It didn't take long for the prison food to become monotonous. Though the dietary allocations had last been amended by the government in 2005, the timings laid down in the Prison Manual for serving the meals remained the same. British-era rules called for all activity to commence only after sunrise and end before sunset. The jail menu and its schedule were quite precise.

**7 am:** 80 ml morning tea.

**7.30 am:** Breakfast of upma, poha or sheera, depending on the day of the week, with 100 ml milk.

**8 am:** Court bhatta i.e. lunch for those scheduled to go to court.

**10 to 11 am:** Lunch or dopahar bhatta for the others: three chapattis, rice, dal and a vegetable, brought one after the other.

**2 pm:** 80 ml afternoon tea.

**3 pm to 4 pm:** Shyam bhatta, the same as lunch.

**4.30 pm:** One banana.

The food distribution was done by the energetic taapa kamaan, one of the many prisoner-teams that play a vital role in keeping the jail functioning. The taapa kamaan were busy from the 'opening of bandi', as wake-up time was known, at around 6.45 a.m., until bandi, around 5 p.m., running around with large food containers—the taapas from which they take their name. Two thousand stomachs demanding their timely due could be a tense proposition and the taapa workers were a harried lot. They had to ensure that every Manual-prescribed item reached each barrack in sufficient quantities to supply the stipulated amount to every prisoner who was present at the morning counting.

Between each meal, the containers had to be cleaned out and readied for the next meal, so the taapa worker knew no rest. Their work was heavy and the smallest mistake or delay could invite curses or worse from the bhais of the barracks. Their only fringe benefit was that they were assured their full entitlement of food, a privilege often denied to those lower down the chain.

The prison kitchen or bhisi worked in two shifts. Modern kitchen equipment could have made these tasks easier, but the availability of cheap and often unpaid labour favoured economies hostile to capital-intensive processes. The only somewhat-modern device was the machine for kneading atta for chapattis. Vegetables were cut by women prisoners. The bhisi kamaan carted provisions from the godown to the kitchen, made the tea, prepared breakfast, rolled and cooked the chapattis, rice, dal and vegetables, and later washed the huge vessels.

Within this unit, the post of taapa commander could be quite a lucrative assignment. The commander was normally a convict warder, a long-serving prisoner who was given the duty of an overseer. He was paid Rs 35 per day, but could earn a healthy side income by trading the resources under his command. By manipulating distribution, he could generate a surplus to be placed on the open market. The bhais who paid him off got more, and better, food. But the taapa commander's privileges paled in comparison with the deals the jail officials struck with the contractors who supplied raw materials to the kitchen. Many middle-level jail employees were able to take enough prison supplies home to feed their families.

These leaks in the supply lines resulted in the depletion of food we prisoners were served. In order to ensure that portions met the stipulations of the Prison Manual, even the most inedible bits of vegetable made their way into our thalis—this could even include the rope suppliers use to tie the vegetables together.

As a result, we were forced to improvize our way around tasteless meals. One way out was to re-cook the food by spicing it up with pickles and chilli-garlic powder purchased from the prison canteen. This process was called handi, after the cooking pots we fashioned out of aluminium plates. We would fabricate a fireplace with bricks or by chiselling and reshaping other aluminium vessels. Strips of newspaper and sun-dried chapattis were used for fuel, but sometimes bits of plastic, dry twigs, old clothes, pilfered prison bedding and even copies of legal documents found their way into the hearth.

Handi was also the term for the group of prisoners who took their meals together. They pooled the provisions they bought from the canteen and foraged from elsewhere. In the barracks, all the members of a handi group (who were called handi-waale) sleep in one place. For people like me, locked individually in different cells, eating dinner together was not possible. Still, we ensured that the food cooked in one cell was passed on to the others. This was managed through a device called the gaadi. The dishes would be placed on a piece of cloth that was dragged along the ground by using a string thrown from one cell to the next, rather like a sleigh.

Work was another way to relieve the monotony of prison. Convicts serving terms of rigorous imprisonment were paid for the work they performed at three different rates, depending on the tasks they had been allotted. But given the meagre wages, everyone was always looking to see what they could skim off the top or the bottom. For instance, the nai kaaman usually dished out military haircuts and bloody shaves. But for friends and paying customers, they could be persuaded to offer varied hairstyles, trimmed beards and shaped side-burns. Such embellishments salved, if not salvaged, egos bruised and battered by the realities of an existence behind bars. Another source of income for those in this kaaman was the sale of shaving blades. Only a few jails allowed blades to be sold in the canteens, because these could be used as weapons. This created an enormous demand for razors from prisoners wary of HIV.

The factory kamaans produced products in the prison workshop that were sold beyond the jail gates. They toiled on power-looms, handlooms, doing tailoring, iron-work, woodwork and even farm work. The jhaadu kaaman was the team with the task of sweeping and cleaning all the common areas such as the grounds and godowns. While the regular team was quite small, their workforce swelled each morning with the forced induction of the naya aamads. Since this new lot could easily be pushed to do free labour of any sort, they were normally put under the jhaadu kaaman, to cut grass, clean, and carry loads. The regular jhaadu kaaman sweepers donned the officious air of supervisors. Choice abuses, dark threats and an occasional cuff on the ears ensured that most of the naya aamads toiled in earnest.

These procedures did not apply to regulars who had made previous trips to jail. They were more involved in re-establishing old contacts, impressing new ones, and arranging for creature comforts for their latest stint inside. These were the kaala topis, a term that arose from the black caps that habitual offenders were once forced to wear. The black cap has been dispensed with but the term is still applied to the canny souls who thrive on their knowledge of the intricacies of jail life. An important aspect of this involved knowing your place in the jail pecking order determined by how long you'd been inside, the number of trips you'd made there, the severity of your crime and, above all, proximity to the bhai.

Each barrack had its bhai to whom all lesser mortals claimed (or aspired to) proximity. Those who managed to get close to the bhai could hope for some alleviation of discomfort in the form of a cleaner or full set of bistar (bedding). Though the Prison Manual prescribed that the bistar allocated to each prisoner should include a dhurrie, a bedsheet, two cotton-wool blankets in winter and a pillow with pillow-case, the naya aamad could consider himself lucky if he managed to get a single tattered, filthy blanket or dhurrie. And even if he did obtain a dhurrie, this did not ensure that the dhurrie-possessor would find the

2 ft x 6 ft floor space needed to lay it out on—because the barracks, designed for seventy-five prisoners, were occupied by more than 200. This was another thing that a bhai could fix.

Since the prime space—against the walls—had already been taken up by earlier occupants, the only space for newcomers lay in the passageway, between the sleepers. As long as others were awake and eating, this passageway was crowded with the activity of those moving to and from the TV, toilet, washing-place and garbage can. It was only late at night, when this traffic died down, that the thoroughfare could be cleaned up and the beech-bistar waale finally wriggle into their wretched spaces. In such circumstances, finding sleep was like chasing a mirage. You almost reached it but were never quite there.

That is not to say that the side-bistars who managed sufficient floor space under the fan or near the window, due to seniority or services in cash or kind, were well off. Harsh lights shining through the night ensured that sleep could never be soothing and relaxed. There were also the regular yells of the night sentries. Despite the barracks being locked at night, security demanded that convict-watchmen patrol the length of the barrack. The jail staff on the outside came by ever so often to check on the sentry and the prisoners, taking care to note the presence of special inmates such as Naxalites and lal topis, literally 'red hats', people who had attempted to escape and were identified by the red arm-bands sewed on their prison uniforms. After reassuring themselves that all was well, they would yell out a list of the numbers: 'Tre-chalees kaidi, ek-sau-pachattar hauladi, athaara Naxalwadi, char lal topi, total do-sou-chalees. Sab khairiyat hain.' This ritual was designed to ensure that the watchmen were not asleep, but provided a steady stream of interruptions to all but the heaviest sleepers.

But even the deepest sleepers sometimes had to surrender to the other sounds of the prison night. With each inmate living through his own private nightmare, moans, groans and sobs from adjoining sleepers were frequent. The awakened neighbour usually slapped the offender into silence. But not all troubled souls were so easily subdued. There were those who pierced the night with shrill screams and shrieks and were usually beaten up before they quietened. The screamer, who actually needed psychiatric help, didn't even get sympathy. As the whole barrack was roused, the more vicious types joined the watchmen in beating and kicking him. Many believed it to be the only possible therapy to exorcise the devil which had taken possession of the troubled man. In a while, he was silenced and relative calm descended once more. But sleep was elusive as each prisoner strained silently to hide from his own demons. As seconds and minutes dragged on, there was no clock to tell the time. Another hour forfeited, never to be returned.

■

By the end of June 2007, the results of the Mumbai narco-analysis tests had come in. They failed to provide any support for the case the police were trying to build so the authorities got the Gondia Court to order another round of tests on Ashok Reddy and me. They obtained this order without informing us, thus denying us the opportunity to oppose it. This time, we were headed to the Forensic Science Laboratory in Bengaluru. The Gondia police decided to transport us there in September by plane. Our arrests had obviously resulted in budgets being increased.

Ashok Reddy and I were transported on consecutive days. The Gondia police had already informed the authorities at the Nagpur and Bengaluru airports of the dangerous nature of the cargo they were escorting. Indigo, the airline by which we were travelling, had been instructed to keep the last five rows of seats vacant. Karote of the Gondia police accompanied me. He was seated right beside me, in the last row. Flying rules did not allow him to carry his pistol. When I was in his custody at Gondia, he'd never miss an opportunity to brandish his firearm, so this made him feel uncomfortable. The other passengers on the flight were initially confused and angry about being barred from using the toilets at the rear. One of the air-hostesses was allotted the job of hiding from them the real reasons for this inconvenience, and apologizing for it. Their arguments kept me entertained through the 90-minute journey. At Bengaluru airport we were received by a team of armed security personnel, the passengers realized I was a VIP or a dangerous criminal. My shabby clothes pointed more towards the latter.

In Bengaluru, the tests were conducted by the notorious S. Malini, who in February 2009 would be dismissed from duty when it was discovered that she'd submitted false papers when applying for the job. Malini was well regarded by police officers across India because she always managed to get them the results they wanted. She had apparently solved the Malegaon blasts case of 2006, the Mecca Masjid blasts case and also the Samjhauta Express train case. All these would later be proved to have been falsely investigated, with the blame put on innocent Muslims.

During narco-analysis, she slapped and abused me, pinched my ears with pliers and administered electric shocks to my co-accused to keep us from slipping into unconsciousness. Her method of conducting these tests was even more barbaric than the procedures followed by the Bombay laboratory.

A report about one of the Bengaluru tests eventually made

its way to the press and I later read the headline: 'Maoist Arun claims that the Shiv Sena supremo funded him.' Malini had asked which organizations I worked with as a student activist. I had mentioned the student wings of various political parties. It is evident that she was not aware of the Maharashtrian Nativist Party and considered its student wing a Maoist front. I imagine that the Shiv Sena and its leader, Bal Thackeray, were as surprised as I was by these findings.

I was brought back to Nagpur by train. Within a few days, Korate had Ashok Reddy and me charged in another case relating to an incident of arson in Gondia. The two activists arrested in Mumbai a little after I was taken in, Sridhar Srinivasan and Vernon Gonsalves, had been arraigned in this case and Korate was generous enough to include us in it too. We were all accused of setting fire to a rail engine in the forests of Gondia.

47

■

### Saturday, 27 October 2007

*I decided to write immediately after arriving from Bengaluru, but then I was taken to Gondia in a new case. I heard from an official at the Forensic Science Laboratory that one of you came to meet me there. The cops did not allow it. Probably they thought you were attempting to abduct and take me home! Try pursuing the Forensic Science Laboratory to give us a copy of the report of their tests. Legally I have been implicated in seven cases till now. In the Nagpur case, the lawyers have filed for bail in the High Court. In the other cases of Gondia, some charge sheets have been filed. The procedure for visiting me is not so simple from what I gather. One possibility is at the Nagpur Court on the date of my hearing. However, the scene out there is a big commotion*

*with many guards, high-profile case, blah, blah, blah. The other*
*possibility is to meet me at the prison. You will be given about 20*
*minutes with a wire mesh between us. You will not be allowed to*
*give me eatables and will have to get an ID card along, as they*
*would want to verify the persons visiting me. Such procedures are*
*only for my type of undertrials.*

*Nights out here are always the time for contemplation. The*
*loneliness compels me to recollect the yesteryears and doze off*
*with those memories. That is the beauty of one's imagination and*
*dreams—no four prison-walls can ever contain them.*

■

By the end of 2007, six months after I'd been arrested, I had
been charged in seven cases: one in Nagpur and the other six
in Gondia. The Gondia cases dealt with Naxal attacks that I
was charged with being part of a conspiracy to plan, or being
part of the group that executed them—or in some cases, both.
Two cases related to incidents of firing between the Naxals and
the police, one was the blowing up of a police vehicle, which
caused the death and injury of a few police staff, another was
of the burning of a railway engine at a crossing, and two were
connected to the murder and beating up of civilians. In all the
Gondia cases, Ashok Reddy and I had local villagers as co-
accused. In two of them, we had the Mumbai arrestees, Sridhar
Srinivasan and Vernon Gonsalves, as co-accused. All the cases
had a maximum punishment of life imprisonment. The police
had filed charge sheets in these cases and now it was left to the
courts and the 'procedure established by law' for me to be tried.

Article 21 of the Indian Constitution holds that 'no person
shall be deprived of his life or personal liberty except according

to procedure established by law'. However this legal procedure—or 'due process' as it is also known—can be easily abused and takes several years to play out.

After being arrested, suspects are to be produced before a magistrate within 24 hours. The magistrate then takes cognisance of the offence and formalizes the detention. In my case, as in the experience of many others, the police circumvented the 24-hour limitation by claiming to have arrested me later than they actually did. In court, the police invariably argue that the investigation of the case requires them to hold the suspect in custody, even if this isn't always necessary. In many cases, especially when the accused has no access to legal assistance, magistrates allow the police the maximum period of custody allowed by the law—15 days. In practice, the police are able to keep the accused person in custody for even longer by arresting them in multiple cases. That's how they were able to hold me in custody for almost a month.

After being arrested and being held in police custody, the accused person is then remanded to prison as the trial proceeds—hence the term undertrial. This judicial remand cannot exceed a fortnight, so the law requires judges to extend custody every time it lapses. As a result, we spent much of our time being taken to court to be produced before a magistrate who would grant this extension and sign a warrant stating the date of our next court appearance. Due to the number of cases in which I was accused, I had court dates around twice a week. The Gondia Court was an 8-hour drive, to and fro. We'd be driven to court, the magistrate would sign our warrants and we'd be transported back to prison.

During this period, the police, now legally called the prosecution, should have been investigating my role in the

49

offences. In each case they filed a charge sheet—a bulky document containing the charges levelled against us—along with the statements of witnesses they intended to rely on. Much of the evidence was fabricated. Then came the process of framing charges, where we, the accused, would have to accept or deny the prosecution's charges. By denying them, the matter would be set for trial and witnesses would be summoned for examination. After the witnesses were examined by the prosecution and cross-examined by our lawyers, final arguments would be made by each side and then the judge would deliver his verdict.

Although the law holds that all these procedures should be conducted speedily, the huge backlog of cases in the courts meant that it would be two years before charges were even framed against us. Producing the witnesses in court caused more delays because the responsibility of serving the summons lies with the prosecution, which had no reason to be hasty about this. Through this protracted process, the judges could, if they chose, allow the accused people to be released on bail. But I was denied this luxury in every case in which I was implicated.

■

#### #1, Monday, 31 December 2007

*I have followed your suggestion and begun numbering the letters I send. In this manner we would know if some letters go missing. Great idea! You can never trust these guys. Whenever I ask the local boss the reason for delay in mail, he blames the postal department. However, I believe otherwise. And have reason for doing so. I enjoyed your visit. Here in prison it is referred to as mulakaat. The time at such mulakaats always seem short for everyone. I am yet to receive the books you gave at your visit. The Guruji is checking them and has decided to give me only two at a time. I am trying to convince him to give me all. Such pleas will probably take time.*

In this closed world, my only window to the outside was provided by books and magazines. However, Maharashtra prisons do not have any funds to buy printed material—not even for official government publications. The prison library is completely dependent on donations from individuals or voluntary organizations. The selections are completely arbitrary, consisting mainly of religious books. At first, most of the magazines I tried to subscribe to by post never reached my cell, especially the ones that were colourfully illustrated. The jailer would decide which books were fit to be read by us. We were once denied a James Bond novel because its cover was deemed obscene. Every now and then, they'd block a magazine because it contained the word 'Maoist' or 'revolution'. I was even denied an annotated copy of the Indian Constitution because it was too bulky.

The employee in charge of all literary, cultural, recreational and educational activity in prison was called Guruji. He was also the custodian of the books in the single cupboard that was somewhat grandiosely described as the library. At first, we had no direct access to the books and would have to request Guruji to open it. A parcha, or chit, would have to be written, duly signed by the jailer in charge of our yard and a guard would then pass it on. After a couple of days, Guruji would then come by, wearing his glasses, and long-sleeved cuffed shirt with its tails spilling out of his trousers. Wiping the perspiration from his bald head, he'd make it a point to articulate his disgust at having been disturbed and tell us how extremely busy he'd been. He suggested that we should have been content to read whatever he chose to send us, instead of picking out our own books.

The total absence of funds limited his abilities to provide many facilities. Guruji would lay out a carom board donated by someone, but not the powder essential for using it. When my family sent me forty books, he saw it as an opportunity to expand his collection. He was also careful about who he lent the books to. Another concession grudgingly allowed by the jail administration was the mulakaat or meeting with family and friends. This was permitted once a month for convicted prisoners and weekly for undertrials like me. Families that managed to save enough money to make the long journey from their village to the jail were expected to first register their names at the mulakaat booth near the jail gate. They would have to wait for three or four hours, braving the sun or rain, as the jail administration would check whether or not they were a security risk or whether they had exhausted their quota of mulakaats. If the limit had been reached, the exchange of a few rupees could fix the problem. After an exhausting wait, the visitors—mostly women and children—would be led in batches into a room with heavily meshed windows, each with a prisoner waiting behind them. On the other side, the prisoners had been warned that they should not exceed the time sanctioned to them. Undertrials got twenty minutes per week, convicts thirty per month. There was always a certain desperation on both sides of the mesh, as prisoners and their families tried to make sure that no important news was missed in the short time at hand.

The first visitors I had in prison were my parents. It had been almost seven months since my arrest. They had left Mumbai for Nagpur the previous day and reached the prison at 6 a.m. However, mulakaat timings started only three hours later. At around noon, the jailer allowed their application, after verifying their identities. Still, I was able to meet them only at 2 p.m. because there was no spare guard in the anda to escort me the 100 metres to the meeting room. At the mulakaat, my parents could only see my silhouette behind the wire mesh. I too could barely make out the colour of the clothes they were wearing. They could recognize me only by my voice. The wire mesh ensured that only voices could be exchanged. No reassuring hugs.

'Were you beaten badly?' my mother asked. Dad sat silently beside her, avoiding direct eye contact. If I were to answer truthfully, it would only cause them more pain.

'No. It's all part of the struggle,' I said, trying to change the flow of the conversation. But even through the mesh, I knew that they'd seen the emotions my smile was attempting to hide. My mom easily understood the language of struggle. As youngsters, we'd debate the virtue of fighting for the rights of the oppressed with her brother, a Catholic priest who was a staunch believer in liberation theology, which interprets the teachings of Jesus Christ to aid the battle against unjust economic, political and social conditions. He had a huge influence on our family.

'How is the food here?' they persisted. 'Is it sufficient? Do they force you to do work?' This was an easier way to introduce them to the operations of the prison.

Although my wife wanted to visit me, we had decided that she should delay her trip because the police had threatened to arrest her too. It would be another six months before she would meet me. My father was keen to travel from Mumbai to attend every fortnightly court date. I opposed it. Willing he was, but I felt that his advancing age wouldn't allow it. We finally settled on twice every three months. We'd plan to meet when I was being produced in court. However, the guards escorting me would occasionally refuse to grant us this luxury. Through my years in jail, my son Akshay never got to see me. We decided against telling him that I was in prison. If he had come, he'd have to see a silhouette with fettered hands for a father. We felt that this would be too much for a 2-year-old child to understand.

My family would try to fill me in about the happenings at home, the talk concerning my incarceration and Akshay's antics as he was growing up. I would amuse them with anecdotes about prison life—the routine prison characters and happenings that are absolute absurdities for an outsider. But as the number of cases in which I was being charged kept increasing, developments in each trial became more confusing and discussing them with my aged parents became difficult. Ultimately, the mulakaats shrank to the ritual of me giving them a list of things I required, and they promising to bring them and also write regularly.

Only five hours each day are allotted for mulakaats, so if a large number of families show up, each gets a shorter visit. Sometimes, just five minutes into meeting with my family, the jail official at the mulakaat desk would start hammering his gavel to signal that time was up. The convict watchman on mulakaat duty would then start banging each window with his stick. To make oneself heard across the dense meshing and above the din of various conversations in mulakaat rooms, it was necessary to yell. As the gavel and stick swung into action, the decibel levels would rise to a crescendo. A wailing child who had been longing for a touch from his father would barely have managed a glimpse of him. A weeping spouse yearning to pour out her heart would barely have got past the initial greetings. A protesting prisoner would not have managed to run through his long list of errands and messages to pass on. All had to be torn away from the windows as the next batch of prisoners rushed in to take their place.

Even lawyers had to be consulted this way. Only prisoners with political or economic clout, and therefore the most dangerous ones, could avoid the meshing and meet their families leisurely, face-to-face in the superintendent's office. The worst affected were perhaps the children, who had to learn to reconcile themselves to a parent penned in a place like the chimpanzee's cage in the zoo. Like so much else in jail life, even the primal joy of meeting a loved one is demeaning and dehumanizing.

■

### #3, Friday, 8 February 2008

*I was taken from the prison and arrested in another case, this time in Chandrapur. The weird thing is that this offence was registered on 6.01.2008 i.e. while I have been in prison. But absurd as it may sound, this is how our system works. During this custody I had no such problems as I experienced the previous time, hence no need to worry. It only makes my stay in jail a bit longer. At a time when Mummy expected that this would be my last year in prison, I doubt that it will be so, knowing the pace at which things work.*

In January 2008, the Chandrapur police had arrested nine members of a students' organization called the Deshbhakti Yuva Manch, for allegedly aiding Maoists. An additional twenty-odd people were detained for interrogation and many more were questioned. The arrested students were booked under the regular mix of charges including sedition, the Unlawful

Activities (Prevention) Act and the Arms Act. These mass arrests created an atmosphere of fear among student-activists and many were forced into hiding. Chandrapur—a district adjoining Gadchiroli—with many coal mines, cement industries and a paper mill, has a history of militant struggles by workers. The Deshbhakti Yuva Manch had built on this tradition and mobilized thousands of students through song, street theatre and a popular Marathi magazine called *College Katta*.

Of late, they had conducted creative campaigns using street plays and poster exhibitions at college gates about the agricultural crisis, farmers' suicides, Bhagat Singh's birth centenary, and more. One set of events in 2005, to celebrate the centenary of Einstein's Theory of Relativity, had proved especially popular with both students and teachers. The events highlighted both Einstein's contributions in cosmic physics as well as his political views. The state seemed to have been threatened by the fact that students had started discussing social and political issues rather than cricket and Bollywood. Despite their efforts, however, the Chandrapur police were unable to establish that the group had any Maoist connection. They needed a certified Maoist as an accused and hence I was implicated. Meanwhile the Anti-Naxal Department headquartered at Nagpur had dispatched petrol-maniac Korate from Gondia to assist the local investigators. He was once again part of the team interrogating me and was probably becoming an expert in how to deal with me.

#6, Wednesday, 12 March 2008

*The temperatures have begun to rise and the trips to Gondia and Chandrapur have started getting uncomfortable. The travel time to each of these places by police van is approximately 3½*

*hours. That makes them full 8-hour outings. The court just gives*
*another two week date and finally I come back, quite exhausted. I*
*know the past nine months must have been horrible for you guys.*
*But let me tell you it was never intended by me and I would have*
*tried my best to avoid it. It so happens that some paths must be*
*taken however burdensome they may be if one believes in a cause.*
*The experience of the past nine months in prison only proves this*
*point. For someone like me, coming from a privileged family, the*
*treatment I was forced to go through is an 'exception', but for the*
*poor this is the 'rule'. Nevertheless I respect your opinion.*

*I recently got a Fredrick Forsyth novel, 'Avenger' and also*
*read Khaled Hosseini's 'Kite Runner'. The western media seems*
*to be all praise for it. The western world's emotional justification*
*for their Afghan occupation. I am presently reading Vikram*
*Chandra's 'Sacred Games', a fictional story on the dons of*
*Mumbai. One finds a lot of similar characters here in prison and*
*especially in anda barrack.*

Salim Sheikh was like a character out of one of the novels I
was reading. His association with the Dawood gang in Mumbai
had earned him a 10-year conviction under the Maharashtra
Control of Organized Crime Act. Salim and Sheikh Rizwan
Sheikh Rashid, a god-fearing Muslim boy from Dhule, who
was convicted for being a member of the Students Islamic
Movement of India (SIMI), were two inmates of the anda
who had enough English novels to satisfy my thirst. Rizwan's
organization had been banned by the government after the
World Trade Center attacks. I considered Rizwan a political
prisoner, like myself. He was arrested in 2001 along with his
father and other youth from his area. While his father died in
prison, Rizwan got a 10-year sentence and by now had grown

a scraggly goatee. Since I shared a hometown with Salim and a political status with Rizwan, we would often meet to review our latest reading. Both of them had a large stock of novels and I was curious about their origin. It turned out that they'd been sent to Nagpur prison by a charity called Prisoners Abroad for a British inmate named Allan Waters.

I first met Allan Waters when he came to the anda barrack every day to clean the wounds my co-accused Dhanendra Bhurule had received from the petrol injected into his rectum. Allan, 63, worked in the prison hospital as part of the requirements of the sentence of 6 years rigorous imprisonment he was serving. He and another British man, Duncan Grant, were former British Navy officers, convicted in March 2006 for sexually abusing minor boys in Anchorage, a shelter they had run in Mumbai. The trial had been known in the press as the Anchorage Paedophile case. During his initial months in the prison he earned a daily dose of verbal abuse, a practice that is quite common for inmates accused of such acts. But over the years, this tall Brit's dedicated work in the prison hospital had earned him some respect. Allan would not hesitate to clean and treat the most ghastly wounds, which even prison doctors would often shy away from. He also had a good sense of humour to ward off all sexual taunts directed towards him and would entertain inmates with conversations in broken Hindi.

Whenever he visited the anda, in his green hospital apron and medical kit, he would make it a point to also bring an interesting novel or magazine. We soon got to chatting in English. I had, by now, got accustomed to befriending inmates accused of moral turpitude. It happened often. Allan would educate me about the workings of the prison hospital and corruption in general. Before his conviction, for almost a year, he had been lodged at the Arthur Road Prison in Mumbai, which for many prison staff was the best place to make an extra buck. The abundance of underworld dons in Arthur Road ensured a constant flow of money for the jailers if suitable services could be rendered.

Allan's stock of novels and magazines from Prisoners Abroad, which was attentive to the needs of British prisoners in foreign prisons, were sufficient to keep the few of us English-language readers occupied. When it came to literature, we couldn't afford to be choosy. Initially, in the absence of books, I'd read two to three newspapers thoroughly every day. Some people in the anda would even read the same newspaper twice or three times every day. The Op-Ed pages were my favourite, substituting for the debate and discussion I craved. Within a few months in prison, as books started coming regularly from Allan and my home, I would spend many hours every day reading. We, the community of English readers in prison, would always find ways to receive books and send them to each other, despite being in isolation. When we could get our hands on them, crime novels were a hit. Lee Child and John Grisham novels would stand in for the courtroom drama we longed for. Friends and well-wishers would send me more serious economic and political journals or books. So fiction and non-fiction would alternate.

Guruji was responsible for arranging for newspapers for all inmates. The Prison Manual stipulated that 'a copy of the daily newspaper in English or in one of the regional languages be provided free of charge for every 20 prisoners or less'. However, the miserly Guruji conveniently ignored such rules and convinced prisoners to purchase their own papers. Every day by 7 a.m., around 100 newspapers would be dumped by the local dealer at the gate, censored by Guruji or the gate jailer and then distributed by a convict to the inmates who had purchased them. If the dealer did not sell a certain newspaper, Guruji would claim that the title was not in the government's sanctioned list of papers. We had repeatedly tried to receive, even purchase, Urdu newspapers but Guruji stonewalled these efforts.

Prison nurtures odd newspaper reading habits. We'd scan the newspapers for any information that could bring us closer to freedom. Hence reports about court judgements were of great interest. Favourable ones could be used in our petitions before the courts or at least incite discussion among us regarding the finer issues of the law. Similarly, news about which judicial bench was hearing bail petitions in the High Court was also vital in predicting the outcome of our cases.

News in prison, like all other things coming from the outside world, is never received in totality. The censorship of Guruji and the gate jailer was a totally subjective process. When Pakistani fidayeen attacked several targets in Mumbai in November 2008, officials at the Arthur Road Prison had decided to keep inmates in the dark and didn't provide newspapers the next day. But the patterns in this seeming arbitrariness soon became clear. Any news of corruption or violence by prison officials would be excised. On some occasions, we received the newspaper in shreds. That was especially the case when we were on hunger strike. Prison inmates, however, had their own methods of getting past this censorship. Those going to court would find out news of what had embarrassed the administration and spread the word through the barracks.

But not all news of the prison department was censored. Occasionally, media people were taken on guided tours and we were allowed to see their photographs and reports about prize-distribution functions of rangoli, art competitions, raksha bandhan melas organized for the families of prisoners to tie rakhis, or examinations on Gandhian thought. But there were days when one could not do any more reading. The mind would revolt and wander beyond one's control. There was no escape but to let those times pass. The best I could do on such occasions would be to observe the ants in the cell for hours on end and envy their cohesive social organization. Then another cycle of voracious reading would soon begin.

# 3.

# Phasi Yard

#8, Sunday, 4 May 2008

*This small note is to inform you all that I am fine. I felt it necessary since you must be getting worried with regards to my health due to the 27-day 'episode'. Overall my health is fine. Details of the experiences during this episode I will reserve for later, when we meet personally, as this medium would not permit it. I can guess the first question that must have come to you was, why did we do it? The answer is simple—injustice is injustice, and needs to be challenged. Something I learnt young. Due to the 'episode', I have been shifted from the anda barrack to the Chhoti Gol—separate. Hence note my change of address. This yard is also called the phasi yard as it is located near the gallows and is the final place a death convict is kept until he is hanged. But don't worry; I have not been sentenced to death. At least, not yet (just joking). In my section at present there are no death convicts. In the other section around eight such convicts are lodged. The gates are closed and we rarely manage to interact with them.*

We were not allowed to write letters or receive mulakaats while on the hunger strike. The Prison Manual prohibited this. Hence my family was kept in utmost anxiety during our protest, which I referred to later in my letters as 'the episode'.

The strike, which started on 7 April 2008, was by political prisoners—those whose acts had been animated by political causes, or who had been arrested because the authorities believed that they held certain ideologies. In this particular case, it had to do with undertrials accused in Naxal offences. The strike was a response to two political prisoners being rearrested immediately after being released from Nagpur prison. One of them was Kusma Mallesh, a mill worker from Surat who had been arrested in 2004 for various Naxal-related offences. Three years later, he was acquitted in all the cases. As he walked out of the prison gate in September 2007, the police arrested him yet again under a 'preventive detention' clause and forced him to spend another 6 months in jail. He was set free on 30 March 2008—only to be detained again under the same clause, but this time in another district. The other political prisoner who suffered the same fate in the same week was Muttakka Naitam, a tribal woman from Gadchiroli.

After hearing this news, I chanced to meet another group of Naxal-accused prisoners on their way to court: Lata Gowda from the women's barrack, and Shyamlal Salame, Sampath Madavi and Fagulal Tekam from the phasi yard. I knew them because we all shared the same lawyer and had been communicating in prison through letters. They were also agitated about these rearrests. We decided to protest with a hunger strike. Like the poor of our country, we had limited choice regarding the form of our protest. During the brief time we were able to confer with each other, we managed to discuss our demands, how we'd stay in communication through the strike, how and who'd contact the other political prisoners, and how information would reach the outside world. The last factor plays a vital role in determining the outcome of any struggle in prison. If news of prison resistance fails to get attention beyond the jail walls, it can be easily crushed by isolating and tiring out the inmates. All communications between ourselves or with the outside world would only be possible by relying on sympathetic inmates to courier notes and verbal messages. We needed a couple of days to make preparations and so settled on 7 April as the day we would commence the strike, four days after our meeting. Back at the anda, my co-accused Ashok Reddy, Naresh Bansode, Dhanendra Bhurule and I quickly worked out the other details before bandi. On 6 April, letters were clandestinely sent to the local press and our lawyers seeking their support.

On the morning of 7 April, we refused tea and breakfast and submitted our demand letters to the state Home Ministry through the prison administration. In this coordinated move, all thirteen of us Naxal accused prisoners from four different and isolated barracks went on an indefinite hunger strike. Our demands were: investigate the recent rearrests, end our isolation in prison; and stop labelling and arresting social activists as Naxalites. We also said that undertrials should not to be forced to wear uniforms. Unlike the rules in other states, the Maharashtra Prison Manual lays down that undertrials accused of murder are to wear uniforms. This was in total violation of the general principle that all undertrials are to be assumed innocent until proven guilty. The United Nations Standard Minimum Rules for the treatment of prisoners also holds that an untried prisoner be allowed 'to wear his own clothing if it is clean and suitable'. We assumed that since our demands were reasonable, the ministry would most certainly agree with most of them and the strike would not have to extend beyond a week at the most.

For the first two days, Jailer Nagdev Pawar did not accept our letters but we refused to withdraw them. They were kept in suspended animation, as the anda barrack amaldar hung them on the barrack entry gate. However, as the news of our protest appeared in the local dailies and made its way to the State Legislative Council, panic struck the prison administration. Four days after our strike had begun, on 11 April, the administration accepted our letter of demands, forwarded it to the home department and within an hour hastily gave us their written replies stating their inability, as per the prison rules, to concede our demands. The ball was now in the court of the state home department. Questions were raised in the Legislative Council and the Home Minister was forced to order an inquiry.

However, as the strike continued, the prison administration slid into passivity. Content with having passed the buck up the ladder, they merely recorded the deterioration in our physical condition. Allan Waters was sent daily from the prison hospital to measure the decrease in our body weight and other parameters. The administration was confident about controlling us using colonial-era strategies they knew so well. As early as 1933, F.A. Baker, Inspector General of Prisons in Punjab, had delineated three systematic stages through which the contagion of hunger strikes was to be treated. The first stage was to immediately separate the striker from other prisoners. This would prevent the strike spreading and break the prisoner's morale. The prisoner was then, in his isolated existence, to regularly and persistently be tempted with food, and his water supply replaced by milk. The final stage was to force feed the prisoner, using a nasal tube to pump down a mixture of milk, augmented by beaten eggs, mutton broth, glucose and sometimes brandy. Nowadays, this is easily done by administering glucose intravenously.

Going without food wasn't as difficult as I imagined. One has to fight the urge to eat only for the first couple of days. After that, the mind and body start getting accustomed to the absence of food and the initial fierce pangs of hunger die down. However, memories of taste would still haunt me. Prison staff would often, especially after bandi when we are alone in our cells, attempt to convince us to eat on the sly: 'Your friends in the phasi yard are eating. Do you want some chivda?' Or they would say: 'Should I get you a biscuit packet to munch on in the night? No one will know' or 'The canteen is selling mutton today. I could ask Salim to send you a few pieces.' Within the first two weeks, my weight started dropping as my body started eating itself. A state of perpetual tiredness started setting in. Even daily activities such as brushing my teeth became burdensome and the easiest thing to do was to lie down, stare at the ceiling and hope that the administration would have a change of heart.

The Prison Deputy Inspector General and City Police Commissioner visited us to observe our condition and try to convince us of the futility of the strike, but no one came to talk about our demands. On the other hand, as an act of solidarity, political prisoners in the Mumbai and Amravati prisons joined our strike too.

About twenty days into the strike, four prisoners were admitted to the hospital because their health had become precarious. Shyamlal, the youngest of us, was already on a drip. We had also received letters from civil liberties organizations across the country expressing their solidarity, promising to intercede on our behalf with the authorities and appealing to us to withdraw the strike considering our health. Ultimately on the twenty-seventh day, faced with an adamant and insensitive government, we were compelled to unilaterally stop our protest. By then, I had lost about 11 kilograms.

None of our demands were fulfilled, and we were fobbed off with promises of 'we'll look into the matter'. Instead, the Additional Director General of Police who was conducting an enquiry into the viability of our demands, advised jail officials to scatter us in the prison. He was also the chief of the Anti-Naxal Department, and was mainly responsible for the policies we were complaining about. Given this support from their superiors in the home department, the prison administration responded swiftly. All of us were dispersed into separate barracks. Ashok Reddy and Dhanendra Bhurule, the journalist, were kept in the anda while the anti-superstition activist, Naresh Bansod was transferred to the gunahkhaana, the punishment yard with solitary cells. I was transferred to phasi yard where the prisoners on death row were kept.

The phasi yard consists of around thirty cells divided into two sections, separated from each other by a guard room and iron gates. The cells in each section are ranged around a small bit of open space. The cubicle with the gallows adjoins the yard, within metres of the nearest cell. I was transferred to the section of the phasi yard in which were lodged some other Naxal-accused prisoners who had participated in the strike, such as Fagulal Tekam, Sampath Madavi and Ganpath Kudmethe, the husband of the rearrested tribal woman, Muttakka Naitam. An additional criminal case was registered against us—of attempting to commit suicide. This was the ninth case foisted on me.

■

#16, Tuesday, 14 October 2008

*The Supreme Court has cancelled the bail of Dhanendra and Naresh. They were brought back into prison. I have yet to meet them. The silver lining is that the Supreme Court, in its order, has stated that our trial should be completed within six months. Our usual court productions nevertheless continue. In the Chandrapur case, our bail was rejected by the Sessions Court. The rest is a big fullstop.*

*Prison was in a festive mood with Ramzan Eid, followed by Dussehra. The Muslim political prisoners in our yard every evening shared their 'iftaar' with us. Sometimes we each received a plate full of fruit and sweets. With such delicacies coming, I easily 'sacrificed' the boring prison dinner. On Dussehra, srikhand was sold in the canteen. Aartis would go on till late in the night. From our yard we could only hear them. Now everyone is looking forward to Diwali.*

*The news of the Kandhamal riots is most disturbing. Christian churches are even being attacked in Karnataka and Kerala. I doubt that things will improve, this being an election*

*year and the need to appease the majority community. What has
been the talk within the Christian community? Do write and
let me know.*

Muslims are represented in prison in greater proportion than in the outside world. In Maharashtra, they account for 36 per cent of the prison population, whereas in society their share is 10.6 per cent. Muslim festivals in prison are important events. During the Ramzan fast, entire barracks are emptied out to accommodate Muslims. Food is served in these barracks at timings suitable for their roza, and prison authorities sell fruit and dates during this month. For those in cellular confinement like the anda barrack, such community gatherings are not allowed. However the cries of the azaan and the sharing of iftaar delicacies lend a festive air to even the anda.

In my section of the phasi yard, Asghar was the only Muslim inmate. He was allegedly a co-conspirator of Javed (who was in the anda) in setting off blasts on the Mumbai rail tracks. Before he was arrested, Asghar Kadar Shaikh, a resident of Mumbai, had worked part-time as an auto-rickshaw driver and the rest of the time as a florist. In jail, he worked as gardener in the compound surrounding the phasi yard. He was also entrusted with the job of keeping the gallows clean, oiled and functioning. Despite the grim task he was expected to do, he was extremely friendly and witty. He always had a unique take on the world around him, and made for good conversation in the yard.

'Prisons will improve only if election rules are changed,' Asghar would often philosophize.

'How come?'

'Once prisoners are allowed to vote, politicians will then pay heed to our needs.'

'You mean, inmates can't vote? But isn't that a fundamental right?'

'Not for us. Hum voting kar nahin sakte lekin chunav ladh sakte,' he answered. (We couldn't vote but we could stand for elections.) He explained how Section 62(5) of the Representation of the People Act, 1951 disqualifies any imprisoned person, whether awaiting trial or convicted, from voting. However, Section 8 and Section 11A of the same act allowed undertrials and convicted persons under certain offences with sentences less than two years to contest elections.

'Dekho,' he went on, 'in slums or villages, the needs of the poor are only fulfilled during general elections. We need to become a vote bank. Politicians would then value our voice and improve prison conditions.'

'But such change will be superficial and short-termed, much like charity.'

'Sahi hai,' he'd continue, 'but it will still be an improvement.'

Debates and discussions with Asghar would continue for days. He often articulated his preference for a death sentence to being imprisoned for his whole natural life. An instant death would immediately end the suffering of his family. It would, he held, allow them to start life afresh.

By June 2008, the number of us in the yard branded as terrorists started increasing. We got three more Muslim boys, Sajid Ansari, Muzzamil Sheikh and Majid Shafi, who had been arrested in 2006 and were accused of planting bombs in a Mumbai train that year. They had been thrashed by the prison authorities in Mumbai and arrived with multiple fractures and bruises. Sajid and Majid were young fathers who had only enjoyed a few months of parenthood before they were arrested. Muzzamil was still unmarried. The three were deeply religious and adherents of Ahl al-Hadeeth, believers in the strict interpretation of the Koran. Sajid and Muzzamil were residents of Mumbai and had earlier been members of SIMI. We had intense discussions on politics and Islam. They despised the Indian state's treatment of Muslims and would never fail to express their views passionately. I had hoped to learn Urdu from Sajid, who was an excellent calligrapher and now regret having failed. Majid, on the other hand, was a romantic. He'd often speak about his family, his baby girl and the football he missed in Kolkata. From our discussions it became evident that Sajid, Muzzamil and most of their numberkaari were arrested merely because of their previous allegiance to SIMI. Majid, on the other hand, was implicated in the concocted police story because he lived close to the Bangladesh border. All of them faced the Herculean task of defending themselves from being convicted of a crime that had left 209 dead and over 700 injured. The well-oiled gallows haunted them daily.

Before September 2009, all the death penalty convicts—including the brother of 'Tiger' Memon, Yakub—convicted in the 1993 Mumbai blasts case had been housed in the other section of the phasi yard. We often exchanged pleasantries and, on festival days, when the jailer allowed us to greet each other, we would talk. However, in the last week of September, after the Bhandara Sessions Court finally reached its verdict in the Khairlanji killings, six of the upper-caste men accused of murdering four members of the Bhotmange family were sentenced to death and brought into our section of the phasi yard. The other two, sentenced to life imprisonment, were kept in the general barracks. I was uncomfortable about sharing space with men responsible for this caste atrocity. But then, in daily exchanges, I had to learn to temporarily ignore their brutalities.

71

These are the compulsions of prolonged incarceration with those most detested by society.

The youngest of the Khairlanji convicts played volleyball and carom with us, while the older men would chat in a corner of the yard, reliving their days under the village banyan tree. In conversations with them, I realized their prejudices blinded them to the enormity of their crime. 'Surekha Bhotmange was to blame. She disturbed the peace of the village,' was their usual defence. They considered her death the logical outcome of the dishonour she had brought to the village. 'She dared to lodge a complaint against us,' they'd assert. 'She was too outspoken and bold, unlike other Dalits.'

'But, did it warrant such treatment and death?'

'It was not planned,' they replied. 'The entire village was angry and the hut suddenly caught flames.'

'Would this same sort of "justice" be given to a woman of another caste?' I persisted. Silence followed.

In other circumstances, such caste violence may have gone unnoticed or at the most would have resulted in the perpetrators being acquitted. Maharashtra has a dismal 3 per cent conviction rate in cases filed under the Scheduled Caste and Scheduled Tribe (Prevention of Atrocities) Act. This time, agitations by the Dalit community throughout the country compelled the authorities to make an example of the accused. In its verdict, the court had concluded that the incident wasn't an act of caste atrocity even while handing down the death sentences to the accused. The failure to prove a case of caste atrocity satisfied the dominant castes, while the death penalty pacified the anger of Dalits. A little later, the High Court commuted this sentence to that of life imprisonment.

Though the phasi yard was home to many people accused

of brutal crimes, the severity of their offences was never a hurdle in confronting the administration to demand medical facilities or better food. On 13 September 2009, all death-row prisoners observed a one-day hunger strike against the death penalty, as part of an all-India campaign to abolish it. No sooner had I told everyone about this than they agreed to participate. In all my experience of organizing agitations on social issues, organizing death penalty convicts was one of the easiest. They had nothing to lose, only a life to win.

■

#17, Monday, 27 October 2008

*I went through your letter. Thanks for believing in me, it really helps. I know I could ask for a copy of the charge sheets in English, but it would just delay things further. I have begun reading the charge sheets of my cases and have already gone through seven of them. The experience however has been quite educative. All the statements of the police witnesses have been written after my arrest and backdated to show otherwise. For staff of their own department, this is extremely easy to do. It is apparent that they have got lower-level staff to fabricate all the statements of these police personnel. The typos and errors made are the same in all despite being on supposedly differing dates. Such would have not been possible if the statements were actually really written on different dates. I thought we could assist the lawyers in preparing points. However, the problem is that the courts don't seem to start proceedings. Now once again it's Diwali time—a time for vacations. Out here we can only hear the sound of fire crackers and we occasionally see a rocket if we sit close to the iron bars. The canteen is selling some sweets…*

*I have 'requested' the prison superintendent during his weekly round about my interest in doing a Post-Graduation Diploma in Human Rights via distance education. He felt examination wouldn't be a problem if they know the schedule and venue in advance, as the concerned court permission would have to be sought.*

The need to force the prisoner to abase himself is built into the administration's DNA.

Even the facilities that belong to the prisoner by right have to be pleaded for. For instance, every prisoner needs to routinely communicate with his magistrate or Trial Court judge. But the mere act of sending these officials a letter is an elaborate procedure. These and numerous other requirements are bracketed into the category of 'requests' that require the sanction of the Prison Superintendent.

This dignitary makes a weekly or biweekly ceremonial tour of the barracks, accompanied by his subordinates, to hear and sanction requests. This tour, which is called the Round, has all the trappings of a guard of honour. A subedar, havaldar and sipahi march ahead of the Superintendent, while other officers slouch along in the rear. The prisoners are expected to line up with a suitably supplicant mien. Those who have a request must step forward barefoot—as required by the Prison Manual—to plead their case. The prisoner is all earnestness and apprehension. The Superintendent's body language speaks of self-importance, indifference and even irritation. Depending on his whims, the prayer is granted or rejected.

Over his time in jail, the prisoner collects experiences like these that ensure that he knows that his place in the hierarchy is right at the bottom—if he's considered human at all. His subhuman status is underlined when the jail is expecting an important visitor, perhaps the Deputy Inspector General or Inspector General (Prisons) or a home department bureaucrat or a judge or a politician. At the slightest whiff of such a round, jail officialdom goes into overdrive. All prisoners are pushed into their barracks and cells and are forced to set up an unnatural display of discipline. Clothes and other belongings are to be piled neatly along with folded bistar and vessels in a pre-ordained pattern. The prisoners are required to squat alongside this display and await the arrival of the VIP.

Meanwhile, officers frantically pace the passages outside seeking to remove the traces of any element known to irritate the visitor's stated aversions. If he's allergic to books, all reading material must go to the godown. If he's known to object to string as a potential aid to suicide or escape, all clotheslines must be dismantled. Nine times out of ten, the visit does not actually materialize. After painstaking preparations, the visitor may cancel his appointment or turn back after a round of snacks in the Superintendent's office. Despite this, prisoners have to suspend all normal work or entertainment for hours on end, and remain in perpetual anticipation. Meal distribution is also put on hold and the hungry prisoners can only hope the 'visit' comes to an end soon.

On the rare occasions that such a round takes place, the visitor and his entourage stroll past the locked barracks and cells while the Superintendent plays the role of guide: 'These are the gallows, this is phasi yard, that is the murder barrack, these are MCOCA prisoners, those are Naxals, that is the bachcha barrack,' (housing young offenders who need to be kept away from adult prisoners, lest the latter's criminal habits contaminate impressionable minds). If the guest is not a high-ranking prison official they usually look around in wide-eyed wonder and peer cautiously through the bars. Occasionally one of them will catch your eye and smile or giggle nervously, perhaps expecting you to bark or growl.

In 2008, I decided to do a post-graduate programme in Human Rights from the Indian Institute of Human Rights, Delhi, by correspondence. My wife had urged me to keep studying. 'Shahid Azmi, the civil rights lawyer from Mumbai completed his law degree when imprisoned under terrorist charges,' she said, 'so why not you?' She contacted the institution in Delhi, got me registered and paid my fees. The syllabus was interesting: I'd be learning about the development of concepts of human rights from the Magna Carta onwards, how they were influenced by the American and French revolutions, culminating in the Universal Declaration of Human Rights by the United Nations in 1948. Reading this in a place with abundant violations convinced me that a mere statement of human rights was inadequate. It had to be accompanied by a struggle for these rights to be implemented. In addition, human rights violations could not be viewed without considering social and state oppression. Such an atrocity-based analysis, devoid of social context, would erroneously equate the rights of the oppressors with those of the oppressed. No doubt, the state officials had their rights, but I'd rather choose to defend those of the citizen.

Though prisoners had the right to do correspondence courses, receiving my course books caused more drama than I'd foreseen. Whenever a parcel arrived by post, the inmate would be required to go to the prison gate and open the package before the gate jailer. On this occasion, when the jailer saw that

I had received forty books relating to human rights, he insisted that the Superintendent certify that they were essential for my coursework. A similar situation had occurred when I received a copy of the Constitution of India from my family during a mulakaat. The Deputy Superintendent refused to give it to me because it was too bulky. It would occupy too much space in an overcrowded prison, he said. Only after a written complaint to his superiors did I manage to get the book, a whole week later. Like all other fundamental rights, the right to pursue academics in prison appeared to be a right only in theory.

The stash of textbooks in my cell became a source of comment. Some inmates wondered whether these books contained legal arguments that would help earn their freedom. To many, my studies were similar to the fasting and prayers that others took up to focus their minds and to pass the time.

While reading the books, though, I noticed how well-founded human rights norms were being diluted. Principles that had been born out of struggle and revolution were being systematically undermined. The no-tolerance posture on torture and state-sponsored assassinations had been turned on its head since 9/11. In the name of countering terrorism, torture techniques used by the CIA, like water-boarding (which resulted in asphyxiation), or political assassinations were being officially patronized. Now, even confessions under duress are being used to implicate the accused. The special anti-terror laws like the Terrorist and Disruptive Activities Act and the Prevention of Terrorism Act permitted such draconian measures. Though these laws have since been repealed, the drastic provisions they contained have been retained in laws enacted by individual states, such as the rampantly used Maharashtra Control of Organised Crime Act, 1999. To use a confession extracted under duress to incriminate the accused goes against international standards established in the Universal Declaration, as also in the Constitution of India. Like the Prevention of Terrorism Act, which preceded it, the Unlawful Activities (Prevention) Act, amended in 2004 to make it even more repressive, also proscribes political organizations and parties. The problem of banning organizations is that it forces proscribed ideologies to go underground and criminalizes any sympathy for them.

However, this has been happening to all forms of peoples' struggles in India—be it the anti-nuclear protestors who were arrested for sedition (one study in 2012 reported that protesters against the nuclear power plant in Koodankulam, Tamil Nadu had 107 FIRs filed against them, implicating 55,795 persons, of whom 6,800 were charged with sedition and/or waging war against the state) or the teenage stone-pelters of Kashmir who were detained under the J&K Public Safety Act (these detentions were documented by Amnesty International and other organizations). Peasants are routinely arrested for opposing a mega-dam, Special Economic Zone or a mining project that has displaced them from their land, livelihood and environment. If a movement chooses to oppose the development model of the state, it soon faces an implicit or explicit ban, a curtailment of its activities and widespread arrests of its sympathisers. Such crude law-and-order fixes don't solve social and political discontent, but merely criminalizes them. Maoism in India is no exception. It is a practice that is incompatible with the fundamental right to freedom of speech, expression and ideology.

■

*Today being Christmas, there was a prayer service for the Christians in prison. It was conducted by a priest and was held at the prison hall. I took this opportunity to go out of our yard and interact with inmates of other barracks. Such chances come only on religious festivals. Post 26/11, the reading of the daily newspapers has become extremely boring. All articles in newspapers and magazines have the same security-centric angle of viewing things. I can imagine what Mumbai must have become, probably a fortress. A similar kind of picture has developed in Nagpur as it is the venue of the state winter assembly sessions.*

At the end of every year, the prisoners are counted up again and all undertrials are given new numbers. The inventory is updated. My hauladi number moved up to 85. Numbers are pushed up when other undertrials are released, explicitly establishing the order of seniority in prison.

79

By now, I had spent 18 months in prison and was much better aware of its rhythms. Practices that would seem bizarre in the outside world became routine behind the walls. For instance, the trapping and hunting of squirrels, birds, bandicoots and other types of small game was a serious occupation because the Maharashtra government had imposed a near-total ban on non-vegetarian food in prison. Even locusts and other insects that occasionally swarmed the prison were collected, to be sun-dried, roasted and relished. Cloth traps sometimes managed to snare a bird. Others were brought down with makeshift catapults. Traps in drain-pipes and other passages could be made to yield bandicoots. But the more popular method for both squirrels and rats was hunting by hand and stick. If one was sighted, the cry went up and the hunters gathered to corner their prey.

A well-fed bandicoot—which tastes a lot like pork—was a sizeable feast for a meat-starved group. It was quickly skinned and cooked in a corner, away from the prying eyes of jail staff and their informants. The spot behind the latrines was considered safe. This was done on the watch of the latrine-cleaning danda kamaan, who are usually low-castes or tribals. They were omnivorous and enthusiastic participants in both the chase and the feast. As the band sat around for the treat, the conversation would drift back to better times. One person would talk of wild boars, another remembered rabbits. The high walls and iron bars would fade away. Things weren't as bad as they seemed.

■

#23, Tuesday, 20 January 2009

*Our mulakaat was very disappointing. We did not manage to get time and I was not produced in court. You must have waited the whole day. I had no method of informing you not to do so. I sometimes think it's better that we do not make plans for such visits, rather than living through the frustration of it collapsing—a waste of time, money and most of all, emotions.*

*The cold has decreased considerably. The yard is now full, i.e. all the cells are occupied. About eight of them are on death row. The latest entrant is a Bihari migrant sentenced to death for rape-murder by the Vasai (Mumbai) Sessions Court. He reminds me of one of the characters of The White Tiger, with all his flirtations with crime and extreme poverty in his village. His antics are presently the centre of all amusement and entertainment. Soon they may become the cause of irritation and quarrel.*

The phasi yard had its own codes. For instance, no one ever

talked about a fellow prisoner's offence casually. If by chance the topic came up, it generated a visible show of emotion. The convict would almost immediately slip into a silent, contemplative mood, which made everyone uncomfortable, or he would go into a rant about why he had been compelled to commit the crime. If the offence was sexual in nature, he would aggressively declare that he had been falsely accused.

Another characteristic of this yard was that everyone was short-tempered and edgy. Small scraps could immediately flare up into physical fights and blood-letting. Continuous residence in the yard, seeing the same old faces day after day, for years on end, kept the convict in a perennial state of irritation and depression. Most of all, the uncertainty was impossible to deal with. Life in the shadow of the gallows left no scope for hope, that essential ingredient that kept other prisoners going. In December 2012, India had 477 convicts on death row.

■

#### #25, Wednesday, 18 February 2009

*With the coming summer we have once again requested that fans be installed in the cells. As usual it was answered by more promises. I am enjoying studying the course syllabus stuff. Although it is vast, I am able to concentrate as it deals with the issues that interest me. The only problem is in giving exams after such a long academic break. The judge is keen to complete the case soon especially after the Supreme Court strictures.*

*Another bit of bad news is that the Gondia police have sought the custody of Dhanendra and Naresh in two offences, nearly two years after their initial arrest. But can we ever dare to question the 'noble' intentions of these 'honourable' men? As you mentioned during your last visit, the economic crisis has severely hit the job securities of the middle class. The poor were always in a state of permanent crisis. The situation went unnoticed as long as it was restricted to the poor. But now with the big financial houses crashing everyone is worried. It's worth consulting the Gondia police; they have the simplest solutions.*

It was very common for the police to rearrest a person for another offence even while he was in prison. This was slightly different from rearresting people at the gate upon release. It made no headlines but the practice was rampant. Some prisoners accused of being Naxalites were implicated in over fifty cases. Prisoners with cases going into double figures were quite common. I've heard of a woman prisoner in the Balaghat district prison of Madhya Pradesh who had more than a hundred cases against her. Keeping track of these cases was an enormously complicated task and following each of their proceedings without competent lawyers was impossible for the majority of the tribal inmates.

Among these political prisoners were Ganpath Kudmethe and his wife, Muttakka Naitam, each of whom were charged in over forty cases. After 5 years in jail, Ganpath realized that he had been arrested and tried twice for the same case. Many political prisoners soon realized that spending several years in prison for one case was not very different from spending the same time for forty or more cases. In fact, the latter situation seemed to be safer because it reduced the possibility of being rearrested after release. Fear of rearrest has caused some prisoners to make applications to the concerned police stations to know which offences they intended to arrest them for in future. Numerous applications under RTI were written to various district police departments, followed up with appeals and then applications to the court to get those cases started.

■

*I woke up in the morning with chronic dysentery. With the monsoons having arrived and the obvious state of cleanliness here, this is at present the most popular ailment in prison. As usual I was prescribed heavy antibiotics. My exams in prison went great. Although, with the sweltering heat, it was extremely difficult to write two papers a day, I somehow managed. The heat in no way discourages the inmates of our yard from playing volleyball. It releases the pent-up frustration, I guess. It also helps build up team spirit in the entire yard. For the death row convicts who never get a chance to leave the yard, a couple of games of volleyball are therapeutic. Now some guys out here want to learn English. I keep trying to dissuade them in learning a language so alien to them, but all my attempts are futile. I now teach a few of them English and Maths. Out here in jail, the fact that one knows the language and is willing to cooperate are the only two qualifications an English teacher requires, given the abundance of students and time.*

83

Passing time in the phasi yard was a major problem. If there was no volleyball, a few would gather to play a game of Ludo or carom. Another would hover around the radio, lost in the world of *Hello Farmaish*, a popular All India Radio show that played listeners' requests. Others would gather near the yard gate to chat with the guards. Some would busy themselves with sweeping and mopping their cells, washing thalis, clothes or bedding, more often than was required. By evening, we would maniacally strut up and down the yard. But this was only possible when the cells were opened, which was for about eight hours each day. The rest of the time, we were by ourselves. While a few would join in the vocals of the radio, others would engage in elaborate handi procedures. Suddenly, someone would break out into shayiri with everyone applauding him. The phasi yard mehfil would come to life.

One Khairlanji case convict kept himself busy killing mosquitoes every night. The walls of his cell would bear the marks of the previous night's kill. Fagulal Tekam, one of the Naxals, and a participant in the 27-day long hunger strike, would sew the elastic bands of old pairs of underwear together to make a ball for the next day's play. Inmates like myself hoped to devour whatever reading material we could lay our hands on.

In phasi yard too, many sought therapeutic trips to the prison hospital to escape the prison monotony. The prison hospital was a great institution, with the Doctor In Charge (DIC) as its presiding deity. The Prison Manual provides the DIC with absolute powers in his field of operation. Whatever the intention of the lawmakers, this has resulted in the rise of a breed of DICs who seem determined to prove the cliché that absolute power corrupts absolutely. The sundry permissions, sanctions and recommendations in the DIC's kitty were all available for a price. Special diets, admission to the prison hospital and referrals to hospitals outside the jail were the more remunerative commodities on offer.

As usual, it was the bhais who cornered the scarce resources. Others who managed some attention were the ones with the greatest nuisance value—loud abuse could often extract something from a DIC chary of exposure. However, those most in need of medical care had to battle it out. But even such a battle wouldn't ensure reasonable treatment.

By January 2010, I won one such battle. It was waged for almost two-and-a-half years and ended with a crown on my left lower molar. This tooth was being treated before my arrest in May 2007, but the prison doctors told me that the only treatment possible was an extraction. It was only after much pleading, requesting, petitioning and quarrelling with the authorities that I finally managed to be sent to the City Dental Hospital to get it permanently filled and fitted with a crown.

However, during the rains, with dysentery and conjunctivitis making the rounds in prison, I needed to be lucky to stay healthy. For medication, I'd have to first pester the jailer to permit me to go to the prison hospital and a guard would escort me there. This would eventually happen by 11 a.m., after almost three hours of constant reminders. At the hospital, crowds would have already gathered to swarm the OPD for their hospital card or to meet a friend. (The hospital is a convenient place for chatting with inmates from other barracks and passing on messages.) An hour's wait with a scuffle or two to reach the junior doctor's desk was only to be expected. As the doctor would usually be late in arriving, I'd wait in the hospital barrack and watch television. Others would amuse themselves with the antics of the mentally challenged inmates lodged in the hospital barrack. I couldn't help but wonder what purpose was served by imprisoning them.

When the doctor arrived, a crowd would gather around him. When I finally managed to get to him to recite my woes I would barely receive a glance. No doctor's touch, no stethoscope or other medical instrument in sight; the physician would silently scribble out a prescription. Treatment was usually determined by the drugs available in the hospital—symptomatic relief and placebos at best, unsuitable and even harmful at worst. I would be escorted back in time for dopahar ka bandi. However, the antibiotic pills I was prescribed would invariably be insufficient. The physician wouldn't give us the whole dose lest we prisoners misuse it to end our lives. But there was no guarantee that I would be brought to the hospital the next day. More often than not, my treatment would remain incomplete, and at the most would nurture germ strains resistant to all but the strongest drugs. The prison medical system has perhaps made its own ample contribution to India's creation of superbugs.

The extension worker of this system of medical care was the nursing orderly. He was one of the jail 'babas' assigned the task of dispensing the available tablets. Besides doling out what the doctor prescribed, he was also supposed to visit the barracks at night to provide medical attention to those in need. This orderly, not having that much pecuniary interest in the services he provided, was often more caring and effective than the doctor at the desk. However, he was limited by the shallow, often distorted, knowledge at his disposal. He often misread, or misunderstood, the character of the drugs he was doling out. Though well meaning, his care carried covert hazards.

But often, medical hazards at night went beyond the abilities of the nursing orderly. If a prisoner got sick at night, the jailer, being the only officer, was quick to shift the responsibility to someone else. Hence, he would order the patient to be shifted to the jail hospital immediately, where the DIC would then become the person in charge. If things became too difficult for the DIC, he would order the patient to be shifted to the government hospital in the city.

Arun Ferreira

This system of passing the parcel often resulted in delayed treatment, as each official hoped that the next person on duty would get down to treating the patient. This occasionally caused the death of the patient in jail. When this happened, a huge cover-up operation would then take place. Intravenous glucose would be injected into the corpse and it would be transported to the city hospital. The official record would show that the patient had left the prison alive, but had died during the journey, before being admitted to the city hospital. In 2010, the NCRB recorded 102 deaths of inmates in Maharashtra prisons, the second-highest figure in the country. Not a single death was attributed to 'negligence or excesses by prison personnel'.

■

#30, Friday, 10 July 2009

*The Nagpur judge is keen on completing the case in time. He has given dates almost consecutively and has been successful in making the prosecution move faster. This is most important. In your absence, another four witnesses were examined; they were declared hostile as they did not testify (in support of) the police version. Two of them were supposed to testify that they were witness to the materials allegedly seized from us, i.e. the pen drive, weapons, literature, etc. Both denied being witness to such an event and said they were made to sign papers at the police station. In short, with these two witnesses the entire prosecution's story has collapsed. It is good news. Four more witnesses have been summoned for the next date.*

*The highlight of this week was my discharge in the 'attempt to suicide' case. In this case, the judge was initially ready to release us on bail. We strongly opposed it, personally arguing before her that we had already completed a major part of the maximum possible sentence under these charges. For us, being released on bail would not translate to getting released from prison due to our remaining cases. I even managed to address the court for almost half an hour arguing how a hunger strike against atrocities should not be interpreted as an attempt to suicide. After hearing me she said that she would commence the trial on the next date. What happened on the next date was most shocking. Rather than start proceedings in the trial, she instead decided to discharge us. Discharging means that the judge did not see any basis for even conducting a trial and therefore relieved us of this case. Discharge is like an acquittal without a trial. The undisclosed factor behind this discharge seems to be the local police headache of producing all of us Naxal undertrials to court for each day of the trial. Arranging such elaborate bandobast for such a trivial matter seemed the larger concern.*

*This Raksha Bandhan I received two rakhis. One from Lata, a woman Naxal undertrial who is the co-accused of the undertrials I teach English. The other is from Dhanendra's sister. Thanks for subscribing to those magazines I had asked for. I have another favour. The problem is we have not been receiving a single copy ever since you paid the money. We have made enquiries out here but they say that they have not been receiving them. I doubt*

88

*whether such is true. Hence do try calling their offices and enquire*
*whether the issues have been dispatched.*

*You were right when you wrote that much of the problems*
*you currently face are due to my arrest and prolonged incarceration.*
*It therefore makes it ever the more difficult for me to advise you*
*given my present situation. I can at the most try consoling you.*
*So, just hang in there. Don't worry, things are bound to change.*
*For me, one of my biggest consolations in jail is comparing*
*myself with the plight of the lesser privileged. Here in prison this*
*perspective is omnipresent. Wherever one looks there is always a*
*sorry case. So whether I like it or not, the society in which I live*
*gives me the strength to live another day…*

Each year, my wife had to remind me of Akshay's age. He, on the other hand, had to be assured by her that I would be coming home for his next birthday. At that age, children live for the moment and though he wasn't totally convinced, Akshay's mind would soon wander off to something more interesting. But the question of his dada's arrival would come up again and again, sometimes even in the middle of the night. My wife found it difficult. Mundane tasks like entering my occupation in his school diary or attending school meetings posed huge dilemmas and my wife sought solutions in her letters to me. She wrote of the challenges she faced at work and at home due to my incarceration and due to doubts about my innocence. She confided that she often questioned the direction in which her life was moving. I had no answers for her.

Initially she had frantically sought information from my lawyers about how long they thought I'd be in prison. But it soon became clear that such queries were futile. Every time an alleged Maoist was arrested somewhere in Maharashtra, my name would appear in the newspapers and things at home would tense up. My family would assume that these new arrests would result in the police filing even more cases against me and that I'd end up spending even more time in prison. But every crisis has its saviours. My brother, sister and the parents of Akshay's friends would strive to see that he did not feel my absence. They would be around whenever he needed a father or my wife needed a friend.

■

### #33, Wednesday, 19 August 2009

*Nowadays the latest craze in our yard has been crafting Diwali and Eid cards. Hence at present my cell is filled with old magazines, leaves and flowers for creating these cards. We craft something like 5-6 cards a day. They are quite a pastime.*

### #34, Friday, 4 September 2009

*In your last letter, you quoted Michel Foucault mentioning the insane roaming free while the sane are locked up. Here's a more relevant and better quotation from that stronger anti-capitalist and democrat, Bertrand Russell— 'Certified lunatics are shut up because of their proneness to violence when their pretensions are questioned. The uncertified variety are given control of powerful armies, and can inflict death and disaster upon all sane men within their reach.' Try matching this one, or do you choose to quit this jugalbundi?*

# 4.

# The Gunahkhaana

#36, Tuesday, 29 September 2009

*Last week two more persons were sentenced to death by the Nagpur Court. It seems to be the most fashionable thing to do. Now since all the 30-odd cells of the phasi yard have been filled I was made to vacate my cell there. I am presently given a cell in the separate yard of Badi Gol, otherwise known as gunahkhaana. Badi Gol would resemble a huge spider from space and I would be in one of its legs. It is the southern octagon meant for undertrial*

*prisoners, as different from the Chhoti Gol—the northern octagon
for convicts. Hence please note the change of my address.*

*In this yard, my two other co-accused, Dhanendra and
Naresh, are kept in adjoining cells. And the other Naxal accused,
Sampath and Fagulal, the tribal boys whom I used to teach
English and Maths are also kept here. Hence lots of familiar faces
and 'family'. Guess October may be the month for the Nagpur
Court judgement. I too have been getting anxious and jittery
about the case as it comes to a close.*

Life in my new lodgings was an improvement on the previous
two prison locations. Although I was still locked up in a cell alone
and technically isolated from the other prisoners, I managed to
meet them, as I began to understand the intricacies of prison
life. For instance, I learnt how to negotiate the mad morning
rush at the tanki or haus, as the bathing tank was known. Four
hundred prospective bathers from two barracks laying claim to
a 60 by 3 foot trough meant a hurried bath even at the best of
times. In summer, when the water being pumped out of the
well was likely to run dry, the pace was frantic. Jail lore tells
of the guy who was not fast enough and had to rinse off the
soap by catching the drops falling off his neighbour's body. The
ones who hadn't learnt to brush teeth, take a bath and rinse
out their underwear in ten minutes flat were destined to scrape
the bottom of the haus. If you wanted to wash your clothes,
you had to forego your bath. Even in the monsoon and winter
months, the water was pumped into the trough only at fixed
intervals and anyone who did not plan his water usage precisely
was likely to be left high and dry.

Negotiating the morning crowds at the tanki and the long
lines at the toilets required not only speed but some presence of

mind. This was particularly important in the yards and barracks with a large number of undertrials who had to get ready to attend court. In less than two hours, between the opening of the barracks at 6.45 a.m. and court call at 8.30 a.m., they had not only to use the toilet and have a bath, but also catch the queues to collect and then consume their tea at 7 a.m., breakfast at 7.30 a.m. and their lunch between 8 a.m. and 8.30 a.m.

It wasn't easy for my body to adjust to the absurdity of having lunch just a half hour after breakfast. The early lunches, like so much else in prison, were the result of sheer callousness. Undertrials often spend the hours between 8.30 a.m. to 6.30 p.m. on their way to court, in court, and being driven back, but the jail authorities did not see fit to provide us a packed lunch that could be eaten in the afternoon. But since the Prison Manual, which governs all activities in prison, laid down exactly what a prisoner must consume, the authorities fulfilled their obligations by distributing lunch to undertrials at 8 a.m. But when you are one among many hundreds running after scarce resources, you normally ended up giving up something—either the toilet or bath, breakfast or lunch.

■

#### #37, Monday, 26 October 2009

*I have just arrived from the Nagpur Court. Once again no witness has turned up. I seriously doubt whether the police served the summons to the two witnesses. I do hope we are produced before the Gondia judge this time. For the past one year we have been going to court, but have never been produced before the judge. His complaint is that we do not reach court on time i.e.*

*in the session before lunch, which is impossible since the police*
*escort party turns up late. As a result the trials have been delayed.*
*We have sent off applications to the Nagpur city police chief to*
*rectify this. However there has been no change in the situation.*
*I am applying for discharge in two cases in Gondia, as there is*
*absolutely no evidence against me. The prosecution has only relied*
*on the alleged confessional statement of my co-accused Ashok. If*
*discharge is granted, it will save me the process of going through*
*the entire trial.*

Another exercise calculated to remind us of our worthlessness
was the recurrent jail jhadati, or searches. Without notice, a band
of jail constables and officers would swoop down on a barrack
and search the inmates' belongings. One night, I was woken up
to the sound of cell gate latches clanging open.

'Jhadati aaya,' whispered Ganpath Kudmethe, the inmate
in the cell adjoining mine. I, in turn, had to pass the news
down the line in case someone wanted to hide something. The
crevices of the wall or the spot under the earthen water gada
were the usual places to be checked. One by one, each barrack
and each cell was searched. After the door of the adjoining cell
was locked, my door was opened. I was made to stand outside
as five or seven guards barged in, supervised by a jailer. Within
seconds, everything was upturned and inspected. With his dirty
boots, the jail staff stomped all over the cell and the bistar I
had carefully cleaned. The feeling of powerlessness and disquiet
while watching my meagre belongings being overturned and
flung to the ground is not easily described.

'Why do you keep so many books and papers?' I had
expected this, but before I answered another one followed.
'Collect his extra clothes. Don't you know civil clothes aren't

allowed?' Containers, twine, curd, extra cloth and plastic glasses got chucked out along with my clothes. The presence of twenty to thirty prison staff around me suggested that any thought of even verbal resistance was foolish.

These searches were supposedly aimed at unearthing banned items. But the definition of banned was ever-changing and depended on the whims of the superintendent, or senior jailer, or even the sipahi conducting the search. Thus an item of food, stationery, clothing or bedding permitted by one officer could become contraband under another dispensation. Legal books would be confiscated because they were suddenly not allowed. After I heard that the police had used the diary maintained by another inmate as evidence in court, I decided to destroy the notes I'd been keeping about my prison experiences, which is why I have had to rely on letters I sent to my family to reconstruct my years in jail.

Of course, prisoners with charas, ganja, mobile phones and other items that were actually contraband had nothing to fear. The bhais would be warned about the raids in advance by the staff. They had good reason to offer these tip-offs. After all, it was the staff that smuggled in these illegal items and had a vested interest in ensuring that nothing got discovered. In jail lingo, they were referred to as 'taxis'. A taxi would arrange to pick up money from family or a friend in return for a standard fee of 40 per cent. Other contraband items were priced differently. Even a mobile phone battery could be charged for a fee. Occasionally, when a tiff broke out between the bhai and the guard, one could assume it was a deal gone sour. However neither party would take the matter higher up for fear that the supervisors would have to be included in the cut. In the unlikely event of contraband being discovered during a search, it would be a minion of the bhai, or even some innocent, who would have to take the rap.

Corporal punishment, though banned, is alive and kicking in Indian jails. Possession of contraband, fighting with other inmates, disobedience, questioning an officer or merely looking him in the eye could merit lathi blows, kicks and cuffs. Gira dena—to fell to the ground—was the term used for the type of treatment many officers meted out. The victim was forced to the floor while a bunch of jail employees pounced on him with sticks, kicks and abuse. A more sophisticated version was naal bandhi wherein the prisoner's legs were thrust between bars and lathi blows inflicted on the soles. The more vicious and energetic lathi-wielders aimed to break a few batons and bones. Often, they succeeded.

The DIC then swung into action—to cover up injuries rather than provide care. He certified that the injuries were minor and did not merit treatment at an outside hospital. Painkillers were administered and the patient transferred away from his barracks into some form of isolation. If he were an undertrial, it would be risky to allow him to go to court as that could mean a complaint there against jail officials. The helpful DIC would be at hand to certify that the undertrial was unfit and could not attend court. This state of affairs would continue until the wounds healed or were at least not visible. Such concealment, however, was not to the taste of all the officers. Many of them spoke nostalgically of the good old days before the spread of awareness about human rights and prisoner rights.

Taksande, our Badi Gol jailer, was one such officer. He would impart to us his views on prison reform. 'Convicts should not be allowed facilities such as mulakaats, furlough or parole,' he'd say. 'It softens their punishment.'

Arun Ferreira

'But is it possible?' I'd ask.

'The courts are to blame,' he would reply. 'In the late 1970s and early 1980s, the Supreme Court held that even prisoners have human rights. And now we have these numerous Human Rights Commissions ever-willing to raise their voice.'

'None of them work, so why worry?'

'Yes. But the problem is that discipline levels drop. No prisoner listens to us anymore,' he would answer rapping his lathi on the table.

When it came to sports, Taksande was an enthusiast. He was an excellent volleyball player and would occasionally join us for a game. But in the evenings, after bandi, he conducted his own brand of physical activity. Any undertrial who had caused a problem in the day was singled out and thrashed by him and the guards. It was common for two to three wooden lathis to break during each session. During his reign, the assaults had become such a frequent practice that inmates began to refer to them as shyam ka bhajan.

In October 2009, Mukesh Chankapure, a bootlegger in his late twenties, was brought to prison. The city's municipal elections were to be held soon and the police dutifully imprisoned such elements to prevent political parties from doling out hooch to potential supporters. It turned out that Mukesh was addicted to his own products and, shortly after being locked up, started getting withdrawal symptoms. He screamed through the night, disturbing the other inmates. The bhais of the barrack had already beaten him twice during the night with the silent consent of the guard. In the morning, with the opening of bandi, it was Taksande's turn. He eagerly performed his bhajan, which consisted of pulling Mukesh violently around by his hand and landing repeated hard kicks with his heavy boots all over his body. Mukesh was then shifted to the prison hospital. He died there early the next morning. His relatives and other members of the Dalit community successfully forced an enquiry by refusing to accept his body. The pressure of forthcoming elections had made it possible. However, the executive magistrate and State Human Rights Commission probing the death were content with the prison's version of 'negligence by the convict in-charge of the hospital barrack'.

Despite this, fractures from such bhajans had to be explained and not all judges were cooperative in overlooking them. Even the superintendent's authority to hand out punishments had to pass elaborate procedures, such as getting a doctor to examine the victim, recording the reason for punishment, sending a report to the courts and getting it sanctioned. Even after all such procedures, punishments like fettering and whipping, though authorized by the Prisons Act, were not appreciated by the courts. Neither is Section 53 of the Prison Manual, which retains provisions for 'whipping to be inflicted with a light rattan, not less than half an inch in diameter on the buttocks' of the prisoner as a form of punishment.

In such circumstances, the best way for the jail administration to legitimately wield the lathi was during an alarm. An alarm was supposed to be sounded when there was a grave threat to jail security, such as when prisoners attacked each other or the staff. But most alarms were planned by jail officers to be used as cover to attack and punish recalcitrant inmates. Sajid, Muzzamil and Majid from the phasi yard had faced such treatment in the Mumbai prison before being transferred to Nagpur.

During an alarm, all the jail officers and lower staff, as well as the convict warders and watchmen were supposed to rapidly bring the situation under control. If there was violence, they were permitted to use minimum force. This was the fig-leaf to justify both wholescale as well as targeted attacks by the staff. At the first sound of the bells, whistles and sirens that announced the alarm, the staff ran wild, swinging their lathis at everyone in sight. Terrorized prisoners ran here and there, trying to escape the lathis and reach their barracks. Anyone outside was beaten mercilessly, driven in and the barracks locked. A count was taken to make sure all were in. As the din and mayhem subsided, the jail officials would start the process of targeted attacks. Those who had previously made complaints or defied the administration were removed one by one from the locked barracks and given a dose of naal bandhi. While some were transferred to other jails, others were moved to solitary punishment cells. These cells were situated in the gunahkhaana that is a feature of every jail, or to the anda barracks, like the one to which I was permanently assigned.

Violence by the authorities in the jails of Maharashtra, like in the rest of the country, is not an isolated event. They are conscious acts perpetrated daily to subdue the prisoner and establish authority. Violence, submission to authority, and discipline are viewed by the prison staff as essential to effective prison management.

On one occasion, in 2010, an inmate was mercilessly beaten in front of everyone in the Badi Gol. The manner in which he was beaten made it clear that he was being made an example of. His crime was that he had jumped over the inner wall of the yard in pursuit of a cricket ball. All the barracks were shut and inmates peered through the barrack gates as the superintendent and other jail officers meted out their justice. The DIC stood by in case things got bloody. Half a dozen lathis were broken, naal bandhi was done but the benefits in terms of discipline were abundant. Taksande didn't tolerate even a defiant silence from an inmate. Prison guards would often praise Taksande for the way he got his barracks locked on time or how he was able to discipline the unruly.

But suppression and subjugation were not the preserve of the authorities. Bhais and some convict warders exercised their powers over other prisoners with almost as much force. Sometimes acting on behalf of the administration, at other times of their own accord, they also handed out punishments of beatings and banishments. Inmates inconvenient to a particular bhai or warder were not allowed to remain in barracks they controlled. Bhais extracted a variety of services from a wide circle. It was not uncommon to enter a barrack and see bhais and convict warders being massaged by groups of young prisoners. The washing of clothes, re-cooking of food, massages and even sexual services were paid for with tobacco, beedis or a goli of charas. One of the warders was particularly notorious. He had first been convicted of a murder done for a ruling party, and while out on parole had followed it up with killing his wife, whom he doubted of being unfaithful. His political connections and long years in jail made him a prison bhai feared by most and he always managed to get a steady supply of young boys to cater to his needs and to share his bistar at night. A big build and stentorian voice aided the image and when he moved in the yards most ordinary prisoners steered clear. He was one of those the jail administration relied upon the most to maintain 'discipline' in the jail.

■

*First and foremost, I must request you that you desist from writing stories of the meat dishes you cook. It adds to my misery (just joking) and brings back fond memories. In this yard too, we have somehow managed to play volleyball. There was no volleyball court, but we cleared up some area of grass and have begun our evening games. Inmates from other barracks too join us and hence we are able to play nearly six to a side. However due to sudden rains the ground has become marshy. We have requested the superintendent to provide us sand. But I doubt whether it will ever arrive. Our 'request' (plea) for a new volleyball itself took almost four months to be answered.*

The condition of sports, recreation and entertainment in prisons is apparent from the state's expenditure on welfare activities of inmates. According to the NCRB, Maharashtra had absolutely no expenditure on welfare activities from 1995 to 2011, except for the year 2010, where a meagre Rs 20,000 was spent. For a state that is among those with the highest number of prisons in the country, such a situation is unnerving. With no expenditure, the administration relies on donations of benefactors and non-governmental organizations. Games such as carom and volleyball are sparingly provided by the prison authorities; however, initiatives for sports or tournaments are generally discouraged on the grounds of security and discipline. In the Badi Gol, we had just one carom board and one volleyball for almost a thousand inmates. Chess pieces had to be privately purchased and playing cards were confiscated during jhadatis. The administration argues they are used for gambling. Similarly, organizing cultural programmes and expenditure on TV sets, radio or video facilities are minimal and depend on the

101

superintendent's relations with donors.

However, inmates would use their ingenuity to cobble a ball together from rags, or smuggle one in on court dates to enjoy a good game of cricket with a wooden bat broken off from a ceiling plank. And when there was a match broadcast on television, cricket fever would bite the whole prison, including staff and officers. Every inmate would be in his barrack, glued to the set. The yards would be empty which seldom happened during the day. In the gunahkhaana, the live commentary would be blasted on the radio. I too was compelled to participate in this craze, since the radio was placed in front of my cell.

In November 2009, Sridhar Srinivasan and Vernon Gonsalves were transferred from Mumbai's Arthur Road Prison to our yard in Nagpur. They had been arrested in Mumbai by the Anti Terrorism Squad (ATS) in August 2007. Like me, they had been booked under the Unlawful Activities (Prevention) Act and Arms Act. However, in their case, the ATS was more generous in planting evidence and claimed to have seized a huge cache of explosives and arms from them. They were transferred to Nagpur on the orders of the Gondia Court. As they were implicated as my co-accused in two cases in Gondia relating to serious charges of arson and murder, our lawyer had applied for them to be transferred to Nagpur so that our cases could be speeded up. They too were residents of Mumbai and well-known activists. We had been communicating by post. Now, being in the same yard gave us the opportunity to catch up and exchange experiences.

Apart from our common experience of arrest, torture and cumbersome litigation, both Srinivasan and Gonsalves, with almost four decades of political experience, had a lot to share. They had become activists in their college days, during the post-Emergency mass struggles in the 1970s and later also became involved in working-class movements. The state could no longer tolerate their dreams of a classless and oppression-free society and had put them in prison. I enjoyed debating contemporary events with both and they, with their warm approach and Marxist acumen, were ever obliging.

Other inmates would easily fail to differentiate between them as they were both tall, had grey hair, glasses, often wore similar styles of clothes on court dates and were always willing to offer legal help. Inmates began referring to both of them as Vakil Uncle. Sridhar and Vernon had been implicated in more than twenty Naxal-related cases in Gondia, Gadchiroli and Chandrapur. Prolonged incarceration, repeated trips to the court, a poor prison diet and lack of proper medical supplements were gradually affecting their health. Nevertheless, they never gave up their daily exercise, selfless service to others and eagerly participated in every prison struggle, including hunger strikes. Despite the government's attempts to quell their spirit , both vakil uncles remained a source of courage and inspiration for many.

■

#40, Friday, 18 December 2009

*Yesterday we finally received the much-awaited acquittal verdict of the Nagpur Court. Although the judgment was expected, it nevertheless brought immense relief and hope. There is still a long road to tread and this news has rejuvenated our spirits. Hope we get more of these small victories sooner. Being the arrest case it further slaps the prosecution on the face with regard to the falsity of the charges they had levelled on us. Last evening we had a small celebration. We all emptied our stocks of chivda and biscuit packets. The local newspapers have carried news of our acquittal, obviously adding their own masala to the events. Do send me the reports that appear in the papers out there. I heard from the authorities that the question papers and answer booklets of my course exams have reached the prison. The exams will be conducted soon.*

My acquittal on 17 December 2009 in the Nagpur case, for which I'd first been arrested, was great news for my family and friends. That case was the foundation of the government's charges against me. The books, pen drives and 'seditious' literature allegedly seized from me could have easily been misinterpreted by the judiciary to convict me. The result of this case would have a bearing on my other cases. This acquittal signalled the beginning of the end. Hope was resurrected and time-frames of possible release calculated. But most of all, the verdict helped in rebuilding trust with my family that had been strained since I'd been arrested in May 2007. I could sense a change in the mood both at home and in the way the media began to perceive me.

My two earlier co-accused from Gondia, Dhanendra Bhurule and Naresh Bansod, were released from prison in February 2010. After the Nagpur arrest, the Gondia police arrested them in two cases of arson. They were fortunate to get bail quickly.

Immediately after my acquittal in the Nagpur case, I applied for bail in the Chandrapur one. My bail application was not heard for almost a month due to the examination of witnesses, and when it was ultimately heard the prosecution opposed it. It was rejected in the Trial Court. I appealed in the High Court, but in July 2010 it was rejected there too. Seven months

104

of unsuccessful litigation since December 2009, just for one bail application. In the Gondia cases, developments unfolded excruciatingly slowly. In July 2009, I had managed to get an acquittal in one of the six cases there. However proceedings in the other cases had come to a standstill because my co-accused, Sridhar and Vernon, had been in Mumbai.

Later, with them getting transferred to Nagpur, things once again started picking up. In the Gondia cases, as most of the crimes dealt with attacks on the police, the witnesses were by and large from their staff. The court would have to repeatedly summon them as they regularly missed dates for testifying, delaying the entire trial as a result. It was only when the judge started getting serious that the examination of witnesses started. Then, by August 2010, I got another two acquittals in Gondia.

By then, I had just two more cases remaining in Gondia and one in Chandrapur.

■

#### #46, Sunday, 14 March 2010

*Regarding the birthday cake you had sent through the gate at your last visit, most of it landed in the potbellies of the person (jailer) you had given it too. He offered me a slice and said, 'Tum khaye ya mein khaye koee farak nahin.' In a sense he respected your desire and also fulfilled his! Corruption takes care of everyone's needs!!*

*I recently finished two brilliant novels, 'The Girl with the Dragon Tattoo' and 'The Girl Who Played with Fire' both are part of a trilogy written by Stieg Larsson. He is a Swedish writer who has written on crime, violence against women and corporate fraud in Swedish society. The sad part is that he died before his works got published. I am sending an article I have written on the proposed Prevention of Torture Bill. Try getting it published; it may help initiate some discussion on this bill, which is extremely important considering its dangerous implications.*

In 2010, the government was planning to introduce a Prevention of Torture Bill in Parliament. I had read it earlier and thought of critiquing it as part of my project work for the Human Rights course. But fear that such a bill would be legislated compelled me to quicken my study. The government had a sense of urgency too. Although it had signed the United Nations Convention Against Torture, 1997, it had failed to ratify it. It also failed to amend the prevailing laws, as obligated by the Convention. However, the proposed legislation was nothing but an eyewash. It diluted the definition of torture in terms of meaning, scope and the punishment for it. It implicitly condoned torture in terrorist-related cases by claiming that it would not apply when the victims of torture were covered by special laws such as the Unlawful Activities (Prevention) Act. Someone like me would not be able to invoke it. This proposed legislation needed a larger debate, especially by civil rights groups, before it was passed.

My article was part of this attempt. Other political prisoners helped me with their experiences and in formulating the issues, and with the help of family and friends, I managed to get it published in time.

In prison, help from the outside is a luxury. It's difficult even to obtain dedicated legal aid from lawyers. Though prison rules allowed our lawyers to visit us, without any restriction on the number of visits per week, we still had to follow the mulakaat practice of talking to them from behind a wire-mesh. This was a major obstacle when we needed to read legal documents. Another problem was that we had no way of communicating with our lawyer if something came up urgently. We could not inform them about a sudden call for police custody in a newly applied case or of incidents of violence in prison, though it is a constitutionally guaranteed right to be allowed access to legal counsel. Other states allow prisoners to make phone calls in emergencies, but the Maharashtra government was still procrastinating on it. At such desperate times, other undertrials were always willing to help. They would, on their way to court, courier a note to our lawyer, or if necessary give him a call for an urgent mulakaat.

■

### #50, Tuesday, 18 May 2010

*Mummy, no need to bring a pair of slippers for me. I have collected two old pairs and have got them repaired with used pen refills. It's a trick I have learnt in prison. In times of scarcity, necessity is the mother of all invention. I also have that pair of sandals you had brought earlier. Only hope my (last) case gets over before I exhaust this stock too.*

*Temperatures have touched 46.7 °C. I am really dreading the next Chandrapur date. Due to the coal mines in Chandrapur, temperatures are usually a degree higher there. It's worth the pain if something happens in court. Even without travelling, the heat is unbearable. Reading becomes impossible with sweat constantly dripping from my forehead. We recently organized a chess tournament in our yard. The league matches are completed and the semis and finals should be held soon. With reading and writing temporarily suspended I have taken to cartooning in full earnest. I am presently working on a collection of characters and scenes which are typical to prison life. Till now I have completed three sketches. I am planning to do a few more. I will have to send them to you.*

On one of those evenings in solitude, when I could not do anymore reading or writing, I casually sketched a scene of Ganesh, the nai kamaan at work in our yard. The following morning, Sridhar, Shyamlal, Vernon and other political prisoners of the yard were thrilled to see my work. They urged me to do some more and suggested that a series of such illustrations would give a true picture of prison life to those outside. I too got excited with this project, which we referred to as 'Colours of the Cage'. I started taking it up as my daily evening engagement. With each new illustration, I got more suggestions and was further enthused. This passion continued for a few months and I sketched over forty such illustrations. However, keeping the illustrations safe in prison was always a challenge. A sudden search by the staff would surely result in them being confiscated. The administration would not appreciate unsolicited prison images of their violations being brought to public attention.

At home, my illustrations had an unexpected effect on my mother. She got depressed on seeing the life I was experiencing, which till then I had hidden from her. Through my letters I had to somehow convince her that though life in prison was on the whole oppressive, one could find ways to relax and even enjoy oneself from time to time. I also assured her that it would all end soon.

■

*More than the heat of the summer, the bigger problem is the virtual non-functioning of the courts. The judge at Chandrapur has returned from vacation, but the witness examination is extremely slow. We have to wait for the Gondia judge to arrive. Hope he does not have a starting problem. My bail matter is due to be heard in the High Court. But I have lost all hope, observing the way it is progressing there.*

*I recently read a book titled 'Superfreakonomics'. I am sure you have already heard about it. It's a sequel to the earlier 'Freakonomics'. I liked it a lot. At the moment there is lots of talk of the transfers of the prison officers and staff. The Inspector General has issued a list. Hence a lot of our present jailers and guards may get transferred. Everybody is doing their own estimations of the possibilities in the Nagpur prison. Some are even trying to alter their transfers by influence or money. We may get a new superintendent in this process. Next will be the transfers of IPS officers in the state. Such transfers had never caught my attention before entering prison. However now being constantly at the receiving end of these guys' policies one starts noticing the change in an individual's influence and thus starts estimating the probable policy changes.*

Prior information of officers' transfers was crucial to predicting our treatment in prison and was often the subject of discussion. Due to archaic prison rules, the subjective whims of prison officials ruled our lives, as I have shown throughout the course of this narrative. The power of these officials permeated every aspect of our lives. For instance, only the jailer of the yard could permit an inmate to write more than the single letter per month stipulated in the Manual. These discretionary powers made daily

109

life in prison extremely arbitrary. While one jailer would allow a visit to the library, another would ask for the Superintendent's permission to be obtained. While one would allow books and magazines to arrive by post, the other would not. The same went for the Superintendent of the prison. While one Superintendent encouraged me to pursue academics, his replacement created numerous obstacles. Hence, a reasonable officer on duty was an essential condition for a relatively peaceful incarceration. Transfers of officers would always upset this status quo and force one to get attuned to the desires and tastes of the new man.

The new jailer assigned to our yard in place of Taksande was a young man who was very soon nicknamed Dabangg. Like the Bollywood character he was named after, this officer regularly trotted around the yard with his sleeves rolled up, swinging his baton. This became even more pronounced if a female jail employee or inmate was in sight. Dabangg would, at the slightest opportunity to prop up his macho image, immediately move into action and pounce fiercely on the nearest hapless victim. This would also be with an eye on making a quick buck from those concerned. A mobile phone unearthed, contraband seized, an urgent message to be passed on or cash to be received meant that Dabangg would collect protection money from all those concerned.

If someone needed to be taught a lesson in discipline, Dabangg would not hesitate to unleash his belt. His style of quick action and apparent justice through such dealings made him popular with many inmates, especially the ones who could pay. Each jailer has his own set of cronies, inmates who would do the deals for extracting money from the victim. When a particular jailer ruled, his cronies had a free hand. Officers' transfers realigned and disturbed these relations too.

■

#58, Tuesday, 7 September 2010

*Yesterday I had gone to Gondia. As usual, summons were not sent to the witnesses and therefore no one turned up. In Chandrapur too, the judge was on vacation and hence I was just given a date.*

*The news of matchfixing has once again cropped up with the Scotland Yard cops arresting Pakistani cricketers. Even in the run-up to the Commonwealth Games many players have begun failing the dope tests. Competition in sport, in this world dominated by money and power, is bound to lead to such episodes. This is only the tip of the iceberg. One of the dons in prison puts it interestingly: 'Everyone does corruption, but it is only the ones who get caught who are called corrupt.'*

For the common inmate, corruption lubricated the inefficient and oppressive prison system. Essentials such as tea leaves for chai after bandi or oil for handi had to be obtained by corrupt means. To obtain cash in jail, your well-wisher outside would have to pay the go-between twice or thrice its face value. Even a cigarette could be purchased through a guard and sold in prison at multiples of its original price. Mobile phones, narcotics and other serious contraband require a more expensive and complicated transaction. The 'carrier', an inmate or guard, would have to be paid, the guards or staff at the gates where the carrier brought it in would have to be managed, and finally an officer would have to be given a monthly sum so that the phone could be used.

Prison guards took money to perform errands, the jailer would make his pile by providing facilities like bedding space, medical treatment or a jhadati-free stay. The higher-ups also had their own methods of feathering their nests, like doctoring invoices or by sanctioning the transfers of prison guards. With absolutely no transparency or protest from the affected consumers, prison corruption was much more rampant and severe than in the outside world. In some instances, the whole hierarchy was involved, with everyone receiving their share. But if by chance the news of a scam became public, everyone had to fend for themselves. Corruption was one of the most common reasons for prison officials or staff being suspended, even though the actual number of incidents of corruption being exposed was extremely small. The responsibility was easily fixed on the lowest ranking prison guard or an inmate.

The prison administration had an absurd way of dealing with corruption. Whenever corruption was unearthed, the service in question was dismantled or curtailed. Inmates, the beneficiaries of the service, would suffer for the corruption of the officials. This was the case with the canteen services and the factory department. In 2009, the Inspector General issued orders to put an end to the almost half-a-century-old practice of selling cooked food by the prison canteen. Weekly non-vegetarian delights sold by the canteen were abruptly stopped. Although Prison Manual rules were cited, the underlying reasoning given was the pilferage of ingredients by staff. Similarly, the factory departments such as carpentry, weaving, tailoring, bakery and shoe-making, meant for training convicts in vocational skills, were gradually dismantled over the years. Even minimal purchases of raw materials could not be done without the sanction of high-ranking prison officials, as it was held that the lower-level staff were corrupt. This resulted in delayed purchases, idle machines and no training offered to convicts. No service was provided and corruption was assumed to have been eliminated. Why not then dismantle the entire prison system? It is horribly riddled with corruption too.

■

*I was glad I cleared all the theory papers in the Human Rights course. I got the maximum marks in the paper on 'Prisoners, Undertrials and Prisons'. I prepared least for that one. Now other inmates have forced me into giving them a treat. I will be purchasing a few litres of milk from the canteen to prepare some sweet. Not officially permitted though.*

*The question of the police rearresting me after acquittal is definitely a fear that I too face. This is the horrible apprehension that every Naxal undertrial goes through. But rather than losing hope and submitting to the seemingly 'inevitable', it is better to work on measures so as to reduce its probability. This year rains have been continuous. One of the guys in our yard has got conjunctivitis. Hope I don't get it. In the separate (cellular yard) we are relatively lucky. In overcrowded general barracks on the other hand, the situation is horrible.*

The problem of overcrowding affects a prisoner's entire life, since it overloads water resources, latrines, sanitation and ventilation. The Prison Manual defines the minimum space allotted to a prisoner in a barrack as '3.71 sq. metres and 15.83 cu. metres'. However in practice, it is normal for three inmates to sleep in the space meant for one. With such overcrowding as well as a noticeable lack of hygiene, contagious diseases have a free run in the barrack. Often, at the tanki, with everyone stripped to their underwear, one could easily observe all inmates of the same barrack having developed scabies or the same body rash.

In October 2010, due to overcrowding in the Chandrapur prison, around sixty Naxal accused undertrial prisoners from there were transferred to Nagpur. All of them were tribals from the interiors of Gadchiroli. With their arrival, I became rather busy. Work expanded to fill the time available. Suddenly, there were always unlettered adivasis from Gadchiroli who required help in sending applications to court, studying their charge sheets or making points for their defence. As most of them were too poor to pay for their own lawyers, they had to depend on the legal aid officers provided by the government. Among such indigent tribals was a young lady, seven months pregnant, who soon after arrival, had been admitted to hospital due to weakness. She later gave birth to a healthy boy in the prison hospital, whom the women inmates appropriately named Azad. Though he had committed no crime, Azad became a prisoner too, and would remain one until his mother was freed.

### #63, Monday, 8 November 2010

*We had a court date today, which was cancelled because the judge is on vacation. I will know of the next date tomorrow. Hope it's a shorter date. I read about Obama's visit to India. It was so hilarious reading the speaker of Parliament instructing the members to behave themselves during his address. She warned them that the way they went gaga and toppled benches during Clinton's visit would not be tolerated this time. She obviously meant such drama would not be tolerated in public, but would definitely be encouraged in private! This drama is best captured by the cartoons and satirical pieces.*

114

*I have started another book by Richard Dawkins: 'Climbing Mount Improbable'. It deals with evolution. He has gone to great lengths to prove how complex mechanisms such as eyes, wings, etc. would have easily evolved down the years. He has relied on computer simulations, mathematics and physics to prove this. It's worth reading.*

*Thanks and sorry for all the trouble you guys went through to send my projects to the IIHR. Because of the contents it would have been impossible to send those articles from here. They would probably land up in some official file awaiting decision for the next ten years.*

*My co-accused and neighbouring cell inmates have just returned from their court date. We have just done some communicating with each other by yelling so that our voices are carried over to each other's cells. He tells me that you have received the drawings I had sent.*

I wrote my postgraduation examinations in prison. It would have been impossible to answer the exam in a hall in the city with a dozen armed guards breathing down my neck. Besides, even if the court had allowed me to do that, I would have had to bear the cost of the security detail. Examinations are usually conducted by the administration in the prison hall, otherwise used for cultural activities. Examinations for inmates are routinely conducted for graduation courses in the arts from an open university. As part of my course, I had to prepare a couple of reports and a thesis. My restricted mobility left me with no option other than choosing issues that were related to prison life. I prepared my field report on 'The State of Human Rights in Maharashtra Prisons', discussing the violation of prisoners' rights in matters like accommodation, bedding, clothing, diet, communication with advocates, family and friends, newspapers, library, sports, recreation, entertainment, production before courts, medical facilities, discipline and so on. My case study report was on the practice of rearrest, titled 'Where arrests follow acquittals', while my master's thesis was on 'Political Prisoners in India'.

Concluding my thesis, my recommendations included: 'The recognition of political prisoners; treatment of all prisoners in accordance with internationally recognized principles, standards and conventions; arrested combatants of armed resistance movements to be recognized, declared as prisoners of war and be treated in accordance with the Geneva Convention; withdrawal of the colonial-era Indian Prisons Act; repeal of special and extraordinary laws such as the Armed Forces Special Powers Act, National Security Act, Unlawful Activities (Prevention) Act, and also of sedition statutes of the Indian Penal Code; an end to the proscription of political organizations; end to all 'false encounters' and 'disappearances' by state forces; unconditional release of all political prisoners and the abolition of death penalty.

I faced a problem sending my work to the institute. In an earlier judgement, the Bombay High Court had held that an undertrial could publish his writings, if they were sent through the prison administration. This judgement was with regard to a book on nuclear physics. My work was much more explosive and even if my legal rights empowered me to do so, I knew it would be delayed endlessly. I passed it on to my family by other methods, methods every undertrial manages to develop in oppressive conditions.

*Great! I have finally completed the course. When I started it I always thought I would be released before completing it. It was good you encouraged me to do it. It helped pass the time and now two years seems to have merely flown by. As usual my yard inmates will expect a treat. Will have to think of something creative this time.*

*Due to the winter session of the state legislature that is held in Nagpur, almost all the 800-odd lifers (convicts undergoing life imprisonment) went on hunger strike demanding liberal rules for premature release. We too supported them. Hence there has been a long line of dignitaries visiting the prison. First the Additional Director General of Prisons visited the jail. He is the senior-most officer in-charge of the prisons throughout the state (below the Home Ministry). After him, the state Home Minister arrived yesterday. As expected the entire jail administration were on their toes. He was supposed to tour all the barracks but ultimately made it a point only to visit the barrack which lodged a corporator of his political party. All this happened of course by chance! And now a day after their visits the entire prison has gone into a virtual sleep mode. The sigh of relief, that everything went well. The important thing is that since the legislative assembly session has now ended our court productions may once again resume.*

117

Maharashtra has more prisons than any other Indian state, followed by Tamil Nadu and Andhra Pradesh. The Additional Director General of Prisons at Yerawada, Pune, is responsible for them. The prison administration is divided into three geographical regions: Western Region, Central Region and Eastern Region. The Nagpur Central Prison comes within the Eastern Region and is the office of its regional head, the Deputy

Inspector General. The DIG, Eastern Region, is responsible for the transfers of prison guards within this zone, an exercise that usually takes place once in seven years. Guards and even jailers often mention the price they must pay if they want to be transferred to prisons of their choice or if they want to be moved before their term is finished. The Nagpur prison is proud of its ISO 9001:2000 certification. Apparently the first yardstick for measuring the bureaucrat's ISO quality is adherence to the colonial Prison Manual.

The prison department along with the police is governed by the state Home Ministry. In 2006, the government set up an enquiry commission for Maharashtra State Jail Administration and Jail Manual Reform headed by Justice S. P. Kurdurkar. It even sought suggestions from us inmates, which we sent. Some prison officers were keen that criticisms of the higher-ups, which figured in most of our points should go to the commission. They themselves could not imagine raising such things as it would be looked on as an act of insubordination. However, after the 26/11 terror attacks in Mumbai, the state Home Ministry reconsidered its priorities, and prison reform was clearly not among them. Among the structural problems to reform is the fact that the police and prison administrations are both controlled by the Home Ministry, which naturally treats the prison department as an instrument of law and order instead of reform. The government did not sanction a further extension of the commission and it wound up without presenting a report.

India's prison policies are security-centric, rather than correctional. The state's priority is to tighten restrictions rather than to upgrade facilities for prisoners. While a broken yard wall would be repaired overnight, it would take three to four months to fix a damaged water pump—and then only if prompted by a couple of hunger strikes. Similarly, laws are passed to make sentences harsher and longer rather than protecting prisoner's rights, and funds are allocated for building more secure prisons, rather than improving the quality of existing ones.

Another hurdle in prison reform is that the higher echelons of the administration are staffed by officers from the Indian Police Service, who do short-term stints in the corrections department. However, they retain their law and order mindset in their new roles. Their approach is mainly to imprison trouble-makers rather than seeking to rehabilitate them.

■

#66, Tuesday, 4 January 2011, 7 p.m.

*This Christmas was better; due to a High Court ruling, we were* 119
*provided with mutton from the administration, for a monetary price of course. And since the price of onions was high this year the resultant dish had fewer. Onions are the usual fillers to proportionally reduce the quantity of meat in the given weighted portion of the dish sold.*

*We were taken to court on both the Gondia date and the Chandrapur one. At the Gondia date nothing really happened as the judge had gone on vacation. I guess he suddenly realized that he had a few more sanctioned leaves before the year's end.*

*The family of another political prisoner regularly sends him magazines and books to read and hence for the present we have sufficient reading material. Among them is Stephen Hawking's recent work 'The Grand Design'. Hence I will send your copy back. My hauladi number this year has reached 5. Only a few undertrials have spent more time in prison.*

*The last Chandrapur date (when we met) was quite memorable. I*
*guess we were in luck this time. Despite the judge not turning up*
*we somehow managed, with some nudging, shoving and coaxing,*
*to get a lot of time to talk. The escort party in-charge was a pain.*
*I managed to have a tiff with him on the way back too. He was*
*so scared and petrified to get us back to prison, that he did not*
*stop even for a urinal break on the way back, despite repeated*
*pleas from the rest of his staff. He was terribly frightened that our*
*van would be attacked and we would be abducted by 'Naxalites'.*
*One gets to meet all sorts of characters in this experience.*

Trips to court were events to which every undertrial looked
forward. They helped break the monotony of jail life and
offered the opportunity to meet one's family and friends. Most
important, they let you find out how far your trial had progressed.
The few moments an undertrial managed to get with his wife
or child would charge him up for another fortnight until the
next court date. On the way back from the Nagpur Court, the
police van would be packed but that would not undermine the
mood. Each undertrial would share the snacks he had received
from his family. Naxal undertrials like us were prohibited from
receiving food from the family. The escorting police team would
be made to sign an undertaking to ensure that we were not
given anything to eat in court. However, on our journey back
fellow inmates in the vehicle always provided us a bite.

But like everything in jail, it took a struggle to squeeze
out such pleasures. The Nagpur police continued the practice
of handcuffing and fettering undertrials to the court and back,
despite Supreme Court directives to the contrary. It took
arming ourselves with a copy of these judgments and some fiery

arguments to ensure that we would not be handcuffed. Similarly, in the court premises, there would always be some officers who would object if we tried to speak to our family or lawyers. Some officers would even prevent our families from attending the court, a clear violation of the law. In the initial years, trips to the Gondia and Chandrapur courts would become extremely disappointing and tiring as my family could not come there and my case wasn't making any progress. The only saving grace was the opportunity to chat with the prisoners from other barracks through the journey as it helped break our isolation.

# 5.

# Hope

My last two Gondia cases were completed in January and February 2011. My earlier attempts to obtain bail having failed, my advocates and I had put our minds to having the trials in my nine cases completed. It entailed studying the charge sheets, picking out anomalies in the prosecution's story and discussing with the lawyers probable lines of cross-examination. It had taken almost four years for all the Gondia and Nagpur cases to be done with. While acquitting me, the judge had concluded in almost all the Gondia cases that there was 'absolutely no evidence against the accused' and that the prosecution had 'miserably failed to prove guilt of accused beyond reasonable doubt'.

I was now left with just one case in Chandrapur, in which I had to defend myself against charges of sedition, membership of a terrorist organization and conspiracy to commit a terrorist act. The number of trips I had to make to court was reduced. My mind now often started contemplating the details of how to hasten the tempo of the process, and how to prepare myself for the future that seemed almost within reach. The same was true of my family. Letters and discussions at mulakaat would always dwell on the probable month of release and possible plans with Akshay and my wife.

#69, Tuesday, 8 February 2011, 9.30 p.m.

*This morning I suddenly received news that I had consecutive Chandrapur dates. So with heightened spirits and hopes we immediately got ready and left. I have just returned and after a quick dinner and some hot tea from Ganpath in my neighbouring cell, I begin this letter. The good news is that the prison administration has begun installing ceiling fans in cells. However it will take some time before they start putting them in our yard. That's the pace of government work when it comes to providing services for the poor. I have read that this summer is going to be much more severe. In one of the articles I read that the Central Government's Model Prison Manual has been uploaded on the net, titled—On Prison Reform & Correctional Administration. Do try downloading it and sending it to me when you visit next. It is not urgent but will help us.*

In January 2011, Dalit writer and cultural activist Sudhir Dhavale was arrested by the Gondia police after he addressed a literary convention at Wardha. Sudhir, a 42-year-old resident of Mumbai, was one of the founding members of the Republican Panthers, an organization fighting for caste eradication in the tradition of the Dalit Panther movement. He was charged by the Gondia cops under the provisions of the Unlawful Activities (Prevention) Act and for waging war against the state. After his time in police custody, Sudhir was brought to our prison and classified as a Naxal undertrial.

I had known Dhavale since my college days. He had always been a vibrant and committed political activist sensitive to the issues of caste oppression. He saw the emancipation of Dalits in the revolutionary transformation of society. From a reading of his charge sheet, I observed that the charges against Sudhir were essentially regarding his authoring and possession of books related to the Maoist movement. As evidence, the police claimed to have seized from his residence a 'Free Dr. Binayak Sen' pamphlet, a charge sheet of one of my cases and books authored by him in Marathi. Although Sudhir published and sold these books legally in Mumbai and the rest of the state, the police booked him in a case in Gondia, more than 1,000 km away. Sudhir's arrest did not go without protest. Many socialists, Ambedkarites, communists, trade unionists, cultural activists, writers and intellectuals of Maharashtra, all united to demand his immediate release.

However the state was getting increasingly thick-skinned. Political activists like Sudhir, Ashok, Sridhar and Vernon were a threat. They exposed the government's anti-poor policies and incited rebellion among the masses. This, the state claimed, was hurting the conducive climate needed to spur investment and the growth of the elite. The armed Maoist movement had to be crushed, regardless of tribal casualties, as its presence prevented the occupation and exploitation of forestland rich in mineral deposits. In the Surjagarh area of Gadchiroli, for instance, steel companies had obtained blocks for extracting huge deposits of iron ore, but Maoist resistance had prevented the mining from beginning. These were conditions that prompted the government to launch Operation Green Hunt, a military offensive against the Naxalites. As a consequence, in the preceding four years, the number of Naxal undertrials in Vidarbha, including tribals of Gondia and Gadchiroli, had quadrupled to almost 120.

As I realized in Nagpur, the majority of the inmates, whether they were alleged Naxalites or not, didn't fit any recognizable definition of criminal. They had landed in jail either because they had been falsely implicated by the police or because of an action committed in a fit of anger, often during a family feud. Not being professionals, they had been convicted due to poor legal advice.

They faced the task of coming to terms with a life they simply hadn't imagined. After the initial shock of conviction, they had to stoically reconcile themselves to living out the long years in jail—which in the case of life sentences in Maharashtra average 17 to 18 years.

A large number found some solace in a rigid schedule of prayer and fasting, puja, namaaz and roza. Prison nurtures spirituality. It has the merit of at least temporarily inducing the type of peace obtained by casting your lot with the supernatural. The sanctimony of ritual has the sanctity of administrative approval. It benefits the prisoner to show up at or even organize religious ceremonies sanctioned by the jail management.

But this game of hide-and-seek between illusion and fact,

between hope and despair, is the constant condition of nearly every prisoner's existence. The trick to be mastered is to ensure that fact does not pierce illusion and despair is not allowed to overcome hope. Once prisoners achieve this, it isn't really that difficult to keep going.

As an undertrial, you tell yourself that the trial's going well, that since all witnesses have failed, you are bound to be acquitted. If you have been convicted, you pin your hopes on the verdict being reversed by the higher courts. In this, the endemic delays of the Indian judicial system are a real blessing. Hope remains alive till your case reaches the Supreme Court, by which time you have reached what you feel should be the end of your sentence anyway. After that, there are remissions and pardons to look forward to.

You enter that bewildered yet hope-filled period of waiting for your likhaan to be finalised. Likhaan is the colloquial term for the review file prepared by the Jail Judicial Department for every long-sentence convict. The likhaan file reports on the prisoner's conduct in jail and contains calculations of the set-offs for which he is eligible. It also contains the recommendations of the jail, police and administrative authorities. This document is sent to the state government for reviewing prisoners' sentences and to obtain premature release. A prisoner usually gets seven days of pardon for every month of his sentence served in jail. Prisoners with life sentences, for instance, are eligible for such mafi and it would be set-off from the prisoner's sentence. The lifer could be prematurely released after 14, 16, 18 or more years in jail. But this pardon is dependent upon his conduct in prison and the nature of his offence. Political prisoners in Maharashta are those who are least likely to be pardoned, regardless of their conduct, and often have to spend between 30 and 60 years in prison.

Arun Ferreira

However, as the government's rules for premature release are so complicated, it is rare for any prisoner to be able to estimate what kind of likhaan he will finally get. It takes years for the bureaucrats at the state headquarters in Mumbai to decide. It is only then that you have some idea of when you can expect to be finally released. This starts your ulti ginthi— the countdown, as you tick off the days remaining for you to go home. Throughout all this, as you battle to maintain your balance. The abiding symbol of hope and despair is the Lal Gate, the red exit gate. It makes an appearance in rhetoric, in small talk, in jokes and in your dreams. It is the barrier that holds you in and the portal that will lead you out. The secret is to ignore the barricade and only see the door. That helps maintain some semblance of sanity.

But for some, the long years of prison life pass without the slightest contact or communication with the outside world. Poverty prevents them from even finding anyone with enough money to put for the surety the state demands for sending a prisoner on furlough or parole. Besides, many families can't afford the expense of travelling to jail for the monthly mulakaat. Illiteracy or the breakdown of family relations could mean that there won't even be a letter. As the lonely years stretch on, the line separating these prisoners from insanity steadily blurs.

Sixty-five-year-old Kithulal was among the victims of such circumstances. His lean, muscular body and hardened palms spoke of a life of toil as a farm labourer, while his long grey hair and feminine gait reflected the community of dancers he came from. He had been convicted for the murder of a small boy who died by accidentally consuming the pesticide Kithulal used for his crops. Kithulal could not afford a proper defence, and now he was denied contact with his family, who lived about 300 km away in another state. He was sentenced to life imprisonment. He would cheat time to give himself hope. He would manage to convince himself that he'd almost done his time and that the benevolent government would be soon announcing a special remission that would see him out of jail. The three or four months before each Republic Day and Independence Day were periods of carefully cultivated hope because he believed that the government would announce an extraordinary reprieve and he would be walking out of the Lal Gate on the great day. As the day came and went, despair would choke his normal loquacity.

He'd then resort to other devices. He would get absorbed in a flurry of apparently irrational activity, as if sweat expended in sufficient quantities could wash away the pain. The normal opiate of fasts and other religious rituals would take on larger dimensions. In a short time, he'd be pinning his hopes on his next release date.

In a place dominated by a few professional felons, Kithulal would put on a show of villainy. At the slightest provocation, he would let loose a loud string of abuse. This amused the professionals. Like kids attacking the a village madman, they'd pelt him with pebbles or insult him, enjoying his reaction. Watching his ranting, I couldn't help but wonder about the sanity of a society that sees fit to incarcerate people like Kithulal for 15 years or more.

■

#71, Monday, 28 February 2011

*The Godhra case verdict is horrible. An attempt to pacify the Hindu majority. Can't decide which is worse—50 persons being finally acquitted after spending 9 years in prison or the ones who have been convicted on the basis of their so-called confessional statement. Now the quantum of punishment is awaited. Based on this logic, I am sure the gallows will be given to quite a few. The Gadchiroli police have halted our escort to court, citing the reason that there is a shortage of guards due to the ongoing anti-Naxal operations. However they somehow manage to provide guards to rearrest from the jail gates, which has become a common practice out here…*

#### #74, Monday, 21 March 2011

*A total anti-climax! After days of waiting, we landed up not being taken to court. Anxiety is on overdrive. Please phone up the lawyers and find out what happened today. Saturday, March 19th was a day of much excitement. Mainly because four undertrials, arrested in Naxal cases got released. Among them was a woman.*

Lata from the bai (women's) barrack and Sampath, Shyamlal and Fagulal from my yard, all of whom had been arrested in Naxal cases, were released in March 2011. They had spent over 6 years in prison. After being released in an initial batch of cases, they had been rearrested in 2009. The court had granted them bail but they were unable to take advantage of the order because they were too poor to raise the money. So they were left with no other option but to be put on trial, which ultimately took more than two years. They too were clients of my lawyer and I had known them since I was imprisoned. All the three boys learnt to read and write in prison. I had been teaching Sampath and Fagulal English and Maths since 2008 and Asghar of the phasi yard had taught Shyamlal. Due to their long incarceration and

129

cheerful behaviour, they were also popular with the prisoners and jail staff. The day after they had walked free, we read in the newspapers that they had been rearrested. Luckily, this turned out to be false. Their release was an extremely emotional time for all of us in the yard. It was a sorrowful yet joyous separation. That's prison life.

In April 2011, the Supreme Court granted bail to Binayak Sen, a paediatrician and human rights activist. He was arrested in Raipur in 2007, a week after my arrest, and similarly charged under UAPA and sedition for allegedly abetting Maoists. An international campaign had called for his release, but Binayak was convicted and sentenced to life. Subsequently, the Supreme Court had granted him bail pending his appeal against conviction. For us, political prisoners it was proof that the charges levelled against us were false.

The Supreme Court made noteworthy observations while granting Binayak bail: 'If Mahatma Gandhi's autobiography is found in somebody's place, is he a Gandhian? No case of sedition is made out on the basis of materials in possession unless you show that he was actively helping or harbouring Maoists.'

We assumed that such a remark would pave the way for bail for hundreds of other political prisoners incarcerated on similar charges. Unfortunately, the Supreme Court did not mention these observations in its written order and hence it could not become a legal precedent. However, the 'Free Binayak Sen Campaign' brought back the issue of political prisoners into the mainstream media and gave a boost to the civil liberties movement in India.

∎

*Thanks for visiting me. I always wonder whether the few moments we get to talk is worth the trouble and expense. Before this visit, I always thought that you had met me only recently. You proved me wrong by reminding me. I think, memories of you guys have conjured up an image of proximity and hence this confusion. There were so many things I wanted to discuss, but seemed to vaporize after seeing you. Next time I should note them in advance.*

*After the last court date did not materialize, I finally picked up a 500+ page novel 'Depths' written by Henning Mankell. The novel is based on a Swedish Navy officer who mapped ocean depths just prior to the First World War. This fictitious character, being mentally sick, pursued adulterous relationships and in the process failed to fathom his own emptiness, finally committing suicide. This author is Swedish. He was, 5-6 months ago, part of a flotilla bound for the Gaza Strip which was later captured by the Israeli authorities. Henning Mankell and other European intelligentsia had undertaken this voyage as support for their struggle of the Palestinian people. Mentioning the Palestinian struggle, you may have heard the good news. The radical Hamas has entered into a unity process with the moderate Fatah faction. It's not yet clear how and why such a unity emerged especially after the various Arab revolts, but nevertheless it is great news and has already frightened the American-backed Israeli ruling classes.*

131

I regularly discussed the Palestinian question with Abbas Mohammed Ali Shahadi, a convict-warder. He was in charge of the danda kamaan and would regularly enter the phasi yard during the cleaning of the toilets for a game of carom or volleyball or to catch BBC Arabia on our yard radio. Abbas, a patriotic

Palestinian, had been arrested in 1998 in a case involving an attack on an Italian pilot at the Mumbai airport. The Fatah-Revolutionary Council, a breakaway Palestinian faction, had initially planned to target an American. But the teenager Abbas ended up shooting at an Italian instead. The Italian survived the attack and Abbas was arrested carrying a machine gun, around 75 live rounds and two grenades. Stories of his experience in jail had all of us enthralled. During the initial years, his hands and feet had been kept shackled throughout the day and it was several years before he was let out of solitary confinement.

Abbas was convicted to a life sentence and after 21 years with remissions, was due to be released in 2009. As his date came nearer, he became ever more restless. His future was uncertain because it wasn't clear that his homeland would accept him. If the Indian government could not deport him, he would be kept in a police lock-up. Fearing this, he regularly made me draft applications to his consulate, the Human Rights Commission and the courts. He even contemplated carrying a copy of Mahatma Gandhi's autobiography on the date of his release to impress upon the police his change of heart. After being released in October 2009, Abbas finally managed only a few months in a lock-up before being united with his sister and ageing father in Jordan. Such stories always brought hope to even the most disheartened in the prison.

■

#83, Monday, 9 May 2011, 6 p.m.

*About the stuff you had sent, the magazines were enjoyed by many and the red ballpoint pens did not reach me. For the prison staff they are invaluable, since in most registers they are required to make their entries in red and the administration does not provide them stationery. Hence, of the two pens, one was pocketed at the gate itself while the other I had to gift to one of the staff for quid pro quo!*

*I have begun reading a book by William Dalrymple—'The Last Mughal'. It is not a fiction piece, rather a book regarding the emperor of Delhi, Bahadur Shah Zafar, and the events of 1857. The story is pieced together from nearly 20,000 documents called the 'mutiny papers' which have never been translated from Urdu or Hindustani. But rather than that boring style of a historical piece, this one is quite light and more like an action-packed novel. However it's nearly 500 pages with a fine font. But what the heck, I have all the time in the world. (At least till the next court date.)*

*Of late we have been enjoying nearly 1½ litre of milk every day. Thanks to our in-charge convict warder who benevolently shares the stuff he manages to siphon off. We use it to make some curd, which is a blessing in the summer.*

Experiencing the dry and scorching Vidarbha summers in prison was a topic that often dominated my letters. Temperatures could go up to 49 °C, as they did in the summer of 2009. Even the electric fans installed four years after I'd been imprisoned merely swirled hot air around us. The switches for both the lights and the fans were placed outside the cell so before bandi, we had to decide whether to use the fan and if so, at what speed. In the cell, the floor got really hot and any attempt to lie on it caused great perspiration. At dawn, ants would climb over me to feed on the salt that had caked my torso and the bedding. I'd wake up every day at about 4 a.m. to their tickle. In the evening we'd have to sprinkle water on the floor to cool the floor. The water situation in the prison was aggravated in the summer. In some barracks the inmates would have to fill drums with water and carry them to their barracks on the first floor. This would take two or three hours every day. Attending to basic needs consumed most of our time in prison.

The monsoons and winters brought other challenges. With the onset of the rains, our ceilings would start dripping and the walls and floors sweating due to water seepage. Each day, with the discovery of every new drip, we'd have to secure a new place for our bedding, books and clothing within the limited confines of the cell. In winter, temperatures would often drop to 6 °C at night, making the cold unbearable. A freezing draft would enter the cell. I had only a single blanket to cover myself with and another to lie on. The only option was to wear multiple layers of clothing. Blankets were in short supply. We once tried to tie old blankets on the cell bars to stop the draft, but the superintendent ordered them to be pulled down. I wonder whether the officials would be able to survive in the conditions they imposed on us. More likely, this was just a way of reminding us inmates who was the boss.

■

#85, Friday, 20 May 2011

*Today, I received a postcard from Daddy. He had sent it from Goa containing this brief message, 'Arrived 30/4 Saturday. Market P.O. We are all well. Thomas.' Daddy's typical short and simple style.*

*We recently commemorated my 'birthday' in prison. Out here, the humour is of very poor quality and hence we stoop to*

*remember our date of arrest as our birthday or entry into the*
*prison world. Hence I have now become four. This day always*
*brings back memories of 8th May 2007. The pain and sorrow*
*could be easily laughed off if this incarceration ended. But till*
*then one has no other option than to grieve. Or sarcastically use*
*the occasion to 'celebrate' and share a biscuit packet with other*
*inmates. I was lucky some of the boys of our yard managed to*
*snare a bandicoot. It was a healthy and weighty one.*

*America seems to have finally eliminated Osama. This head*
*of Osama may help boost the electoral chances of Obama in the*
*next presidential elections. He has been facing severe criticism*
*from the right-wing conservatives regarding the health reform and*
*bailouts for corporates and hence needed this kill. While America*
*claims that they have given a fitting reply to the killings of 9/11,*
*one wonders whether the same feeling of vengeance is allowed for*
*all the victims of the wars in Afghanistan, Iraq and now Libya.*
*Wars that were unilaterally engineered by America. But these*
*questions we aren't supposed to ask, lest we too are labelled as*
*'terrorists'!*

America's Islamophobic policy was a topic Salaam, a senior convict, enjoyed discussing with us when he'd come daily to our yard for a bath. His wisdom was built from years of reading literature while working as a typesetter in a printing press in Chandrapur. Salaam was convicted to life imprisonment for a murder he never spoke about and details of which I could never bring myself to ask him. Now, as a warder, convict overseer, he was in charge of distributing the letters and money orders we'd receive by post. The mail would be delivered at the prison gate by the afternoon and it was 60-year-old Salaam's job to collect it, inform the prisoner concerned, acquire his signature and present him before the jailer for the letter to be censored.

In the case of money orders Salaam had to acquire the prisoner's signature before depositing the receipt back with the gate jailer, who would then enter the amount in the prisoner's account. This job meant knowing every prisoner and their barrack and Salaam was extremely efficient at it. While others would have to shout the name of the concerned inmate, Salaam would do this with the least effort, like a true dakiya. Suddenly he'd be near you, wherever you were in prison, peering over his reading glasses to inform you about your letter. Before bandi, we'd often eagerly look out for him, because to sight Salaam meant a letter had arrived. He was finally released in 2011, after spending more than 17 years in prison.

Salaam only needed a wee nudge to get talking as he washed his clothes.

'The Wikileaks exposure of the US diplomatic cables has exposed America,' I'd start.

'For Islamic nations, their dadagiri was always visible,' was his prompt reply.

'And now the US has pounced on Assange.'

'Woh toh hai.'

'Many have also come out in support.'

'This wouldn't be possible if Assange was a Musalmaan,' commented Salaam. 'He would have been easily labelled a terrorist, denied support, isolated and ultimately physically eliminated.'

Salaam's conclusions were always thought-provoking.

■

#88, Sunday, 24 July 2011, 5 p.m.

*The rains have picked up here too. We experienced continuous*
*showers for the past 4-5 days. The water levels in the prison wells*
*have risen and hence the water problem has been solved, until the*
*next summer of course. The Mumbai bomb blasts were horrible*
*as you rightly said—too many innocents killed. Gujaratis were*
*especially targeted. However in prison I have had the opportunity*
*of interacting with some guys who believe such blasts to be correct.*
*They cite the events of the 2002 Gujarat riots, where innocents*
*of the Muslim community were targeted, raped and killed. They*
*incorrectly blame the majority Gujarati community for such*
*crimes against humanity. By doing so, they fail to see the role*
*of the rulers who engineered these riots as part of their policies*
*of divide and rule. They thus fall into the very trap created by*
*the real perpetrators. Though their anger and want for revenge is*
*reasonable and justified, their methods are misplaced. The State*
*too has horribly failed in protecting their lives. While the major*
*players of the Gujarat riots roam scot-free, the most devoted of the*
*Muslim youth are arrested and made to rot in jail.*

*Don't worry; we maintain 'safe distance' from the eunuchs*
*in our yard. There are many characters in prison such as druggies,*
*peddlers, and other professionals, who we have learnt to stay away*
*from. They too have no interest in socializing with us, except for*
*an occasional court application that they request us to draft. Other*
*than these guys, who are the usual frequent visitors to the prison,*
*there are the majority who have committed an offence by accident*
*or compelled by circumstances. They are the better elements to*
*socialize with.*

In July 2011, three young eunuchs Sonia, Sapna and Saloni,
accused of a murder were brought into our yard. The prison
authorities could not send them to the women's barrack nor

keep them in a general barrack lest their presence provoked sexual attacks on them. The anda barrack, phasi yard or similar cellular confinements like ours were the only option. These cells are out of bounds for the other prisoners, but we soon had a steady stream of visitors from the other barracks—they had devised some excuse or the other to enter and catch a glimpse of the new entrants. As my cell was before theirs, many would stare or make a pass at me assuming from my clean-shaven face that I was one of the eunuchs they were searching for. Angered by this, I even contemplated growing a moustache. Suddenly our yard which was earlier inhabited mainly by us political prisoners became the centre of attraction for all inmates. For us too it was a learning experience—we soon made friends and, as the three got talking, we gained first-hand knowledge of the severe stress and strain that society imposes on the LGBTQ community. Such strain increased manifold in jail. They had landed here after a quarrel that began when they were soliciting alms in a train turned horribly wrong and one passenger was killed. Denied bail, they had to spend 18 months in prison as undertrials, before they were acquitted and walked free.

Somehow my last Chandrapur trial proved to be a test for my nerves. It was the case where I had been implicated with the youth of the Deshbhakti Yuva Manch. A case designed to resemble those grand conspiracy cases of the British Raj and proving to be equally messy. I would grow anxious as this last court date neared. In October 2010, I had court dates on every alternate day. I expected my acquittal and release by December 2010. An unexpected bonus was that my co-accused, local students from Chandrapur, would manage to treat me to delicacies unavailable in prison. One day it would be homemade mutton masala, on another it would be sweet-pumpkin pakodas or egg masala. A series of such consecutive dates invariably gave me a stomach upset. Eating the same insipid food in prison had made my intestines sensitive to rich and spicy food. Not that I cared.

Then suddenly for the next two to three months, the pace slowed down. The judge went on vacation and witnesses were not turning up. In March 2011, the Nagpur police stopped escorting us to court. Was it better that we were not compelled to undergo the 8-hour long journey in the scorching sun when nothing was happening in court? Police personnel informed us that our court dates had ceased because the government had not sanctioned a diesel allowance for the escort vehicles. The official story, though, was that guards were not available due to security concerns.

When we began to be taken to court again in May 2011, another delay arose. After the trial had proceeded for nearly four years, the judge decided to add another recently arrested person who was wanted in the case to our trial, thus making way for his trial to be heard with ours. This would mean that although witness examination in our trial had concluded, it would have to start afresh. My lawyers and I fiercely resisted this move. I took the opportunity to speak in court and explain to the judge how this was a method regularly used by the prosecution in nearly all my cases. The police would show a list of nearly sixty-seventy accused, delay their arrest and when arrested, propose that they be added to the trial. Each addition of an accused person to the trial delays the trial. The cops would deliberately use this strategy to incarcerate us indefinitely.

The judge was soon convinced. Then in July 2011, we stopped being taken to court once again. Police bandobast had been increased in the city due to communal unrest and both police personnel and the vans for our transportation to the court were diverted. The case was stalled again. It wasn't until 18 August that the judge finally recorded our statements. The arguments of the prosecution and the defence soon followed. This roller coaster case would have concluded in August but then the judge went on vacation. I was confident about being acquitted. It was the delays that made me anxious.

■

#91, Wednesday, 31 August 2011

*Hi, where would I have been in different circumstances? Just can't stop dreaming. It was horrible to hear that the judgement was not pronounced yesterday. Throughout the days leading to the 30th I have been distributing my belongings, which is the practice in prison. Anyway, the events of yesterday once again confirm my faith in the ineffectiveness of our justice delivery system. Our judge did not pronounce his judgement because he did not go through the papers and a long date was given because he is now going on vacation. I have to now submissively accept my deprivation of liberty till he comes back from vacation and reads the case papers. As always, do I have a choice? This delay has happened in all my previous cases. Why didn't I expect it this time?*

There is a 'prison-release routine' or rather tradition that every inmate follows religiously as his day of release approaches. I would anxiously wait to hear my name called out by the convict warder assigned this duty. As soon as the barracks opened, I'd wait for him to appear. All morning ablutions and meals had to be planned so that I wouldn't miss his call. When I saw him, I'd try to read his lips, in case he was too far away for me to hear his yell. Once my name was called, another process would begin—meeting inmates and exchanging hugs with all who had been friends and 'family' all through my period of incarceration. As I started to gather my belongings, another set of inmates would crowd the doorway—the type who wanted to lay their hands on my belongings. There is a prison superstition around this routine: it holds that all clothes worn in prison should be left behind or else bad luck will follow. One was expected to walk out in a new set of clothes. Still, though habitual offenders followed this practice rigorously, it could not guarantee that they would not return a few months later. Thereafter, I would be given a meal and sent off to the judiciary department of the prison for release.

#### #92, Thursday, 8 September 2011

*Mummy, I heard you had a fall on your way to meet the lawyer.* *Hope it's nothing serious. At this age your bones, especially at the hips tend to get brittle. I guess you had too high expectations about the last court date. It's better to expect the worst and therefore be mentally prepared for whatever the outcome. Like I mentioned in my earlier letter— 'there's many a slip between the cup and the lip'. This would include all the events from the court date, judgment, and release from prison, until reaching Mumbai. It's better to be prepared for the worst. Although my personal experience tells me it's easier said than done. Nevertheless, try it.*

*If all works out well, we could plan a trip out in the Diwali vacations. Akshay too will enjoy it. I have not received a letter from you. Regarding your plans to come and visit me I suggest 24th September. In case the judgement is not delivered on that day, you may have to cancel your trip and book it for the next court date.*

Prison wisdom says that the first few months of jail life and the last ones are the most horrible. And as freedom neared, the days grew longer and I would lie awake at night. Reading and writing became extremely burdensome. Old school and college friends popped up in my dreams. My mind was probably preparing itself for life on the outside. I started making plans for the future. On 24 September 2011, the Chandrapur court finally dismissed the last of the nine cases against me. Immediately after the order, I managed to phone my wife using a friendly police officer's mobile. She appeared shocked to hear my voice on the phone after almost four years and initially thought that my call meant that I had been arrested in yet another case. Extreme joy is impossible to express to one's wife over the telephone, especially on a cop's phone, surrounded by half-a-dozen armed policemen. That would have to wait.

# 6.

# Lal Gate

On the morning of 27 September 2011, I received a mulakaat from my lawyers, mother and brother. We excitedly discussed all that I would do after my release. I had informed them that it would take a couple of hours to complete the procedures for securing my release before being able to meet them. By 2 p.m., all those to be released were lined up before the Lal Gate. I was deliberately kept as the very last.

As I stepped through the wicket-door, a group of men pounced upon me. I could not see my mother or lawyers, who,

I later came to know had been made to stand beyond the outer wall of the prison. I attempted to scream and alert them, but the men had their hands clapped on my mouth and, pushing down my head, they dragged me out of the gate. Within seconds they dumped me into an unnumbered white Tata Sumo that had been parked a few feet from the gate. Six men jumped into the vehicle and I was driven out of the prison premises. My mother, brother and advocates, who had come to receive me, were pushed out of the prison by the authorities. My lawyers immediately went to the local police station but the cops there refused to register a complaint regarding my abduction. It was obvious that personnel from the police station and the prison authorities had assisted my abductors.

I was taken out of the city. My abductors, who I assumed were policemen, were armed and refused to disclose their identities, the purpose of my abduction or our destination. I pleaded with them to ease my family's anxieties by informing them or my advocates about my whereabouts. They refused, despite having mobile phones on which they were receiving repeated instructions from their seniors. After about three hours, I was taken to a police station in Gadchiroli district.

The police rearrested me in two more cases related to Naxalite attacks in 2007 and I came to know my abductors were policemen of the C-60, the elite commando force involved in anti-Naxal operations in the Gondia and Gadchiroli districts. I was once again produced before a magistrate, who granted the police custody despite my complaining about my abduction and rearrest. After five days in Wadsa Desaiganj, Gadchiroli, I was sent back to the Nagpur prison. My old companions in the gunahkhaana had come out to the Badi Gol gate to receive me. Each of them hugged me and helped me settle back into my old cell, filling me in on the details of reports of my rearrest that had appeared in the newspapers. I was crushed at the thought of having to run through the same cycle of torture, bail applications and waiting endlessly for trial dates.

■

#93, Tuesday, 4 October 2011

*Hi, the tiger ultimately bared its fangs, I guess!! Or rather the true face of Indian democracy. All through the journey after I was rearrested from the prison gates I kept wondering about what you two would be going through. Though I was mentally expecting this, I nevertheless kept hoping against it. Hoping that I would be able to join you. Guess such dreams and plans will get postponed. But however hard they may try it will definitely happen one day. I came back into prison on the 3rd at around 4.30 p.m. I received tremendous support and sympathy from everyone—inmates and lower-level staff included. All have offered some suggestions, help and instilled hope. In fact, throughout this entire episode it is the state which has discredited itself and sacrificed long term interests for short term ones. It has reduced people's confidence in the judicial system.*

*All inmates chipped in to make sure that my life was restored the same as prior to my 27th September rearrest. I have been given the same cell, beddings, buckets, etc. These essentials I have been gradually accumulating throughout the past 4 ½ years (defended and safeguarded from numerous prison jhadatis) and it would have been a pain to start from scratch again. This was one of my major fears which was easily solved by the love and affection of other inmates—like a family you could say. I also heard that 125 inmates observed a day of hunger strike in protest of my rearrest.*

*And finally, an attempt to answer the most important question that would have crossed your minds—how much more time to go? One thing is sure that it wouldn't be as long as the earlier period of 4½ years. So don't be too disheartened. The lower time limit is based on many factors, but such would be best discussed in person rather than writing via this censored medium. I am sure this opportunity will soon come.*

My rearrest was not an exceptional act, particularly in relation to Naxal cases in Gadchiroli district. The desire to show results and win awards and increased funds was leading police officers in Gadchiroli district to increase the number of persons shown to be arrested as Naxals by detaining released prisoners at the jail gates. Many prisoners, particularly poor tribal villagers who lacked adequate legal defence, were abducted from jails at the time of their release with the connivance of prison officials. In the records, the abducted people were shown to have been arrested anew in some remote corner of the district.

In prison, I met three tribal men from Gadchiroli named Baburao Narote, Kejuram Pudo and Vilas Kallo who were rearrested at the jail gate every two or three months—each time they were released. After their first arrest from their village in Dhanora, Gadchiroli they were released on bail in October 2011. On release, they were abducted by cops in civilian clothing outside the Chandrapur prison but on the way to Dhanora, the police van transporting them had a serious accident. Three other tribal men from their village who were also rearrested were critically injured with spinal injuries and were hospitalized for over a month. Baburam, Kejuram and Vilas were put back in prison, this time in Nagpur, with bruises and fractures. Within two months they were again granted bail. But on release, they were arrested for a third time, in December. By then, their families had run out of money to pay for bail so the men had no choice but to reconcile themselves to a prolonged stay in prison until the completion of their trials.

Despite my disappointment, my rearrest had a silver lining. It brought this obnoxious practice of the Gadchiroli police to national attention. Newspaper headlines said, 'Is Maharashtra becoming a police state?', 'When the State Turns Abductor', and 'SC guidelines violated in arrest of Ferreira outside Central Jail.' It brought the issue of my incarceration back into focus. Family, friends, media persons and civil rights activists who had campaigned for my release suddenly started receiving overwhelming support. Civil society groups and individuals who had earlier refused to give their overt support started coming forward. I even became an issue for political rivals to compete on. City level leaders of both the ruling and opposition parties made representations to the Home Minister and Director General of Police demanding my immediate release. By arresting me again, the credibility of the state had taken a beating.

This round of police custody in Gadchiroli was completely different from my earlier experience in 2007. The police were not at all interested in interrogating me or keeping me in custody. They merely wanted to show on the record that I, the 'dreaded terrorist' was 'severely interrogated' to prejudice the judiciary in ensuring that my incarceration be formalized by due legal procedure. In fact most of my time in the lock-up during this stretch was spent in reading a John Sandford novel.

In October 2011, the prison administration suddenly transferred many Naxal undertrial prisoners to Amravati, ostensibly because our numbers were increasing. I feared that I too would be transferred. Transfers from one jail to another are so arbitrary and abrupt that they are a major cause of anxiety. Suddenly, you would get a message from the judicial department of the prison that your transfer had been decided and the police escort had arrived to take you. You were then expected to pack up without any discussion and leave. Such transfers were usually used by the administration to crush potential dissent. In this particular case of Naxal undertrials being transferred to Amravati prison, the ones who were the most vocal in raising issues with the authorities and who had relatives in the women's barrack were targeted. It became obvious to us that the recent hunger strike by men and women inmates was a cause of concern for the administration. We had collectively protested the brutal assault of Angela Sontakkay, a woman Naxal-accused, by the prison staff.

An analysis of the trend of these transfers brings to the fore another hidden motive of the government. Earlier in October 2010, around sixty Naxal-accused Gadchiroli tribals were transferred from Chandrapur to Nagpur, a distance of more than 180 km from their villages. Then, in October 2011, they were transferred from Nagpur to Amravati, 330 km from their villages. In 2012, a few were transferred to Akola, more than 430 km from their homes. The government was hell-bent on severing all their ties with their community, so as to cripple their legal defence. It won't be long before we see tribals of Gadchiroli lodged in the prisons of Mumbai.

When re-admitted in prison I was assigned hauladi number 162. Due to the increase in the number of undertrials arrested in Naxal offences, the administration had begun classifying and numbering us separately. I was the 162nd Naxal undertrial to be admitted in the Nagpur prison in 2011. This number had grown from just thirteen in 2008. Throughout my years of incarceration, it was this community of political prisoners that became my de facto family. A desire for social change and a common approach for struggle kept us united in prison despite being lodged in different barracks.

In the rest of the country, too, we political prisoners now formed a significant proportion of the non-criminals in jails. As people across the country increasingly confronted the ruling classes and their state, our numbers were rising. While all of us shared some conviction in a cause dreaded by those in power, many of us had been implicated in acts in which we had played no role, or acts that had been criminalized by the provisions of special laws. Muslim students who protested communal atrocities, tribals who fed a Naxalite squad, activists and Maoist sympathisers could all be labelled terrorists and anti-nationals under a variety of special laws.

149

Such political prisoners entered the jail with a stamp imposed by the police that the prison authorities immediately acted upon. Their first step was a quarantine policy that was followed more stringently than any Prison Manual provision for communicable diseases. Segregation was the rule and the greater the estimated ideological infection the prisoner could cause, the harsher the segregation. The anda barrack, gunahkhaana cells and even phasi yard came in handy to cut us off from ordinary prisoners. We Naxalite prisoners were listed separately in the daily counting and forced to wear green sleeve bands to mark us out. In July 2007, the Inspector General of Prisons issued circulars on how to contain Naxalites and restrict their influence not only on prisoners but also on the prison staff and officers.

In all this, he was only faithfully adhering to the 'septic tank principle' proposed by Reginald Craddock, Lt. Governor of Burma, in his correspondence with the Indian home department in 1918. He prescribed separate barracks, separate yards and even separate prisons for freedom fighters to 'keep the poisonous gas within the tank and ensure the safe custody of those emitting it'. Despite the Supreme Court ruling against the quarantining of such political prisoners, prisons across the country routinely adhere to this practice. The new 'Model Prison Manual' of the central government even calls for the setting up of separate and isolated 'high-security' prisons to lodge such inmates.

But try as they may, no jail administration can hold back the fragrance of the septic tank from reaching the barracks. As I've said earlier, every day, much of our time went into teaching those interested in learning English and Maths, drafting legal applications or translating English case papers into Marathi or Hindi. This earned us credibility so when we organized agitations, such as the one in October 2009 to protest the death of Mukesh Chankapure, the bootlegger who was beaten to death in prison, the prisoners immediately heeded our call to boycott the day's meal. The authorities knew that political prisoners had the potential to unite everyone in a just cause. A sizeable section of the general barracks had also joined our campaign in February 2010 to support statehood for Vidarbha.

The Naxalite and Muslim political prisoners joined hands on 13 September to commemorate the martyrdom of Jatin Das, who died on the 63rd day of a hunger strike, along with Bhagat Singh in the Lahore prison, during the freedom movement. In jails across India, this day is observed as an occasion to demand recognition as political prisoners and call for their unconditional release.

But, as I have tried to show in the book, the life of a

political prisoner is a lonely one—the loneliness accentuated by memories of a more productive existence outside. Political prisoner yards are oases of silence, in contrast with the otherwise crowded and noisy surroundings. The scrape of a chess piece or click of a carom striker are often the only sounds. Many choose to immerse themselves in day-long reading and desultory writing. But these too are perhaps forms of escape from reality, quite comparable with the delusions of the 65-year-old long-haired Kithulal.

■

#96, Sunday, 13 November 2011

> *In case you have not heard the good news, I have been ordered to be released on bail in one of the two cases. After the formalities of producing sureties are completed, I shall be released in that case. However there is no immediate need to rush this procedure, since the other case is still pending. It should end by this month or latest by the next. Hence I am not trying for bail in it. The news of bail is really refreshing. Suddenly life in prison merely seems to be a bad dream.*
>
> *I recently read a good novel by Jeffrey Archer, 'Prisoner by Birth'. Interesting to read how the British courts work and the conditions of the prison there. The story is a modern version of 'The Count of Monte Cristo'. At present, other than the usual responsibilities of reading others' charge sheets, I am going through another novel by Henning Mankell, 'Kennedy's Brain'. Not action-packed stuff, but a touching story of the practice of anti-AIDS serum trials in Africa.*

In November 2011, my dedicated team of lawyers in Mumbai,

Nagpur and Gadchiroli finally got me a bail order. My lawyers were not only efficient and capable but were also committed to getting me through the colossal tangle of cases, which at times seemed impossible and hopeless. As civil rights advocates, they viewed the incarceration of political prisoners as reflecting the undemocratic state of affairs in the country. They were always ready to defend our rights and would, whenever the need arose, rush to the High Court or the Gondia, Chandrapur or Gadchiroli courts despite repeated threats and annoying surveillance from the police. Shahid Azmi, one such civil rights activist and lawyer, was shot dead in February 2010 at his office in Mumbai at the young age of 32. The deeper links of his supari killers were never investigated. Shahid had been a relentless defender of political prisoners, especially of Muslims arrested in terrorist crimes and was part of my legal defence team in Mumbai.

During prison struggles or hunger strikes, these lawyers would immediately respond to our call and provide all possible support. In emergencies, they would also arrange to provide stationery, legal literature, clothes or even just visit my family to console them. Indeed, over time I began to regard my lawyers as family.

■

#### #97, Wednesday, 23 November 2011

*The news of my bail was reason to celebrate. Today we 'arranged' for a special dinner. We bought some extra milk from the canteen and made srikhand on the sly. So for dinner it was srikhand and prison roti. Heard a Tintin movie has been released. Wonder how Captain Haddock uttered 'Blistering Barnacles and Thundering Typhoons'.*

*The judge was on vacation and hence we have got another date after almost a month. Therefore release plans may be further delayed. Hope this delay gives the lawyers adequate time in preparing my petition to be filed before the High Court regarding my abduction and subsequent rearrest. It may be necessary for you to be in touch with the Mumbai and Nagpur lawyers, as an affidavit may have to be prepared stating on oath that you were present at the spot of my abduction. I heard that the local government officials have been harassing you for a bribe for the preparation of the solvency papers for my surety by stretching a process which can be done in a few minutes to almost two weeks. Once they sense there is urgency and anxiety they tend to be more greedy. Sarkari vultures never miss out on such opportunities. Hence be patient, we have time until the other case is completed.*

153

# 7.

# Beyond the Lal Gate

On 3 January 2012, my advocates filed a petition on my behalf before the Nagpur bench of the Bombay High Court seeking remedies for the violation of my fundamental right to life and personal liberty. It sought compensation, action against the police officers responsible for this outrage and an enquiry into the practice of abduction and rearrest of undertrials like me by the Gadchiroli police. I had been acquitted in ten of the eleven cases I had been arraigned in and was granted bail in the last one of Gadchiroli. This last case related to an incident of firing between Naxals and police personnel in the forests of northern Gadchiroli.

The next day, 4 January 2012, I was to be released. My parents had come a day earlier to submit the bail papers in the Gadchiroli court and would remain to receive me after the court ordered my release. But, stepping out of the Lal Gate once again made me extremely nervous. From the morning, I had been looking for signs of another possible rearrest. This time, I packed my toothbrush, some toiletries, a set of extra clothes and some stationery. I would need them if I was rearrested and sent to another prison. Chandu, the danda kamaan of the anda whom I met on my way to the judicial department, assured me that this wouldn't happen. He received this information when he had gone to clean the toilets in the staff quarters. Even friendly guards and employees informed me that there was no police activity outside the gate. Nevertheless, I doubted my release would be trouble-free. Fortunately, the vociferous public outcry and the skills of my lawyers worked in my favour. After 4 years and 8 months, I walked out of the Lal Gate, a free man.

155

As I stepped out, I was greeted by my mom, dad, advocates and journalists.

'It's over,' I said, hugging my parents. I had no comments for the eager media, wary that anything I said would be used against me. That's what happened in November 2010 when Tusharkanti Bhattacharya, a political prisoner from Andhra Pradesh, was rearrested after a few months based on an interview he had given to the media when he was released.

We returned to Mumbai the same day. Throughout the journey, my mother was extremely nervous every time we passed a cop. My sister too had instructed her not to let go of me until I got back home safely. My Nagpur advocate repeatedly rang me to check whether all was well.

The next day, at home, I began receiving calls from friends and well-wishers. Mom became my temporary personal secretary. I had to write a letter to Vernon and other friends at the Nagpur prison as I had promised. Mistakenly, I wrote my own address as Nagpur. I mentioned getting home safely and how I was enjoying a simple but divinely tasty home-cooked meal. Later, I met my wife and Akshay, who was now turning seven. He had just come home after giving his school tests.

For a moment, he failed to recognize me. 'That's Dada,' my wife helped him.

'So how's my Ben-ten hero?' I said to break the ice. From prison, I would occasionally draw him a cartoon and send it to him in my wife's letters. He had pasted these on the door of his cupboard. The cartoons did the trick. He was soon talking to me, sitting on my lap and telling me about his favourite cartoon character.

'How did your maths paper go?'

'Hmm, okay, but I got one sum wrong,' he answered, gradually getting comfortable with the idea of conversing with a Dada he had no previous memories of.

As the conversion started picking up, halfway through a sentence he abruptly asked, 'When will you be going again?'

I answered him with a hug.

Over the next few days, my family told me about events in Mumbai related to my arrest: the flood of allegations appearing in the media; the unexpected police searches and visits; the hostility they experienced from persons earlier considered well-wishers; and the new friendships built on true sympathy. But rather than these events, what they were more interested in talking about were the trials and tribulations they had been put through, the emotional distress they had to deal with. During these past years, my parents had aged considerably. My incarceration had had a large role to play in this. My brother and sister had selflessly put in their best efforts to help me, sacrificing family commitments and putting their jobs at risk. My wife too, had kept her life and career in a state of suspension, juggling multiple responsibilities in my absence.

I was relatively fortunate. After his release, Naresh Bansod had to deal with the collapse of his marriage. His boy stayed with him, while his daughter lived with his former wife. Dhanendra Bhurule and his wife somehow managed to get back their earlier jobs and repay pending loans. To the best of my knowledge, Ashok Reddy is still incarcerated in a prison in Andhra Pradesh.

For the longest time, I found it difficult to deal with my life as a free man. Persistent phone calls from the media left me in a daze. In prison, the only person I would meet was my lawyer and we would always jot down in advance what was to be discussed with him. Technology, too, was a big challenge. In the world of apps, mobiles and other gizmos, I felt challenged. All this made me realize how totally unsuccessful prisons are in preparing a person for society. Being in jail for 4 years and 8 months temporarily incapacitated me. I wonder how those who are released after 18 to 20 years cope with life on the outside.

Habits learnt in prison die hard. I often get that urge to preserve a used pen refill so I could repair a pair of broken sandals or a plastic container for our handi gaadi. Solitude, too, is something I miss from time to time. The occasional hustle or noise at home or at get-togethers soon makes me irritable. I also get nostalgic for some aspects of the simple prison life, such as the camaraderie I shared with other political prisoners and the depth of friendship and solidarity we were able to develop. The abundance of time we had at our disposal allowed us to understand each other almost in totality.

∎

Life after prison is weighed down by two emotions. One is fear—the fear of further action by the State. The fear that the State will somehow get me back in the prison, as has become prevalent with those political and human rights activists who have chosen to dissent. The fear that Big Brother is watching every step I take, watching who I meet and watching which peoples' struggle I choose to support. My involvement in any such movement will then become an excuse for branding it Maoist and justify repression.

The second is the emotion of confusion—of how to build life back again, how to build those relations that were tested and strained during the years of incarceration. Confusion of how to live life and yet follow the ideals I believe in. To sacrifice the latter in the interest of the former is much easier. However, I guess all these dilemmas are part of the freedom every other citizen experiences in this so-called democracy. This freedom is definitely better than a caged existence. This freedom however needs to be worked on. Yes, it needs to be worked upon.

# Acknowledgements

Any expression of gratitude would be incomplete without appreciating the efforts of those who worked for my release.

To Dad, who never for a moment stopped believing in me till his end. To my mom, sister, brother, their families, and Jenny—who spared no effort for my release despite the difficulties. Their support and encouragement will always remain invaluable. And to Akshay, for giving me the reason I needed to start sketching in prison.

Many thanks to P. A. Sebastian, Susan, Maharukh and members of the Committee for the Protection of Democratic Rights; those 'Friends of Arun' and other well-wishers who campaigned for my release; Surendra Gadling, Anil Kale, Pradeep Mandhyan and members of the Indian Association of People's Lawyers who defended me and continue to do so.

This book would not have been possible without the ever-willing help of Naresh and Vernon. Naresh, for painlessly making me relive the experience, extracting the most out of my pen and for tirelessly and patiently helping me build the manuscript. Vernon's contribution or rather participation has been indispensable. He took it up as his own.

Finally, a thanks to Jerry Pinto for all those pointers and comments, and to David, Aienla, Simar, and others of the Aleph team who, in many small and not so small ways, demonstrated a strong belief in the need to publish my book.

160

Arun Ferreira

# APPENDIX

Details of the arrests, charges, trials and acquittals

## 8 May 2007

My initial arrest constituted the creation of a conspiracy case at Deekshabhoomi, Nagpur.

The offence was registered at Dhantoli police station, Nagpur on the day of my arrest and I was charged and tried under provisions of the Unlawful Activities Prevention Act. My acquittal in this case came on **17 December 2009** by a Sessions court of Nagpur.

## 28 May 2007

Implicated and arrested in a case of blasting of a police vehicle near Bevartola dam, Gondia.

I was charged and tried for murder, criminal conspiracy, rioting, possessing of arms and under provisions of the Unlawful Activities Prevention Act. A Sessions court of Gondia acquitted me in this case on **13 August 2010**.

## 6 June 2007

Implicated and arrested in a case of the murder of two youth at Ganutola, Gondia

I was charged and tried for murder, criminal conspiracy, rioting, possessing of arms and under provisions of the Unlawful Activities Prevention Act. I was acquitted in this case on **5 February 2011** by the same Sessions court of Gondia.

## 14 June 2007

Implicated and arrested in three more offences of Chinchgadh police station, Gondia.

Two of them were cases of firing on police parties. In both, I was charged and tried for attempt to murder, rioting, possessing of arms and under provisions of the Unlawful Activities Prevention Act. I was acquitted in these two cases on **11 June 2009** and **19 July 2010**. The third was a case of assault in Sukdi, a village in Gondia. Here, I was charged and tried for attempt to murder, voluntary causing hurt, rioting, possessing of arms and under provisions of the Unlawful Activities Prevention Act. I was acquitted on **13 January 2011**.

## 20 October 2007

Implicated and arrested in a case of burning of a Railway Engine at Toya Gondi, Gondia.

I was charged and tried for attempt to murder, arson and under provisions of the Railway Act and the Unlawful Activities Prevention Act. I was acquitted in this case on **13 August 2010** by a Sessions court of Gondia.

## 29 January 2008

Implicated and arrested in a conspiracy case related to the Deshbhakti Yuva Manch, Chandrapur.

This offence had been registered at Ramnagar police station, Chandrapur on 6 January 2008 whilst I was in the prison. I was charged and tried along with other youth from the Manch for criminal conspiracy, sedition, under provisions of the Unlawful Activities Prevention Act, Press Act and Arms Act and finally acquitted on **23 September 2011** by a Sessions court of Chandrapur.

### 25 July 2008

Arrested in a case of attempt to suicide relating to the Hunger Strike we observed in prison.

Our hunger strike in prison was registered as a crime of attempting to commit suicide by the Dhantoli police station, Nagpur on 20 April 2008. The Magistrate court of Nagpur after coming to the conclusion that a hunger strike does not constitute an attempt to suicide, discharged us without a trial on **20 July 2009**.

### 27 September 2011

After my release I was abducted at the prison gate and shown to be arrested in a case of firing on a police party in forests near Zhendepar village, Gadchiroli.

This offence had been registered at Purada police station, Gadchiroli on 22 February 2007 and I was charged and tried for attempt to murder, rioting, criminal conspiracy and for possession of arms. I was acquitted on **30 December 2011** by a Sessions court of Nagpur.

### 30 September 2011

Implicated and arrested in a case a firing on a police party in the Jafragadh Hills of Betkathi forest, Gadchiroli.

Here too, the offence had been registered at Purada police station, Gadchiroli almost four and a half years prior on 24 April 2007 and I was similarly charged and tried for attempt to murder, rioting, criminal conspiracy and for possession of arms. Two years after my release on bail, a Sessions court of Gadchiroli acquitted me in this final case on **29 January 2014**.